Staff Performance: From Appearance to Interactions

By

Dr. Salwa Elmeawad

Preface

In today's rapidly evolving professional landscape, the success of an organization is increasingly reliant on the cumulative performance of its individuals. Whether it's the first impression left by an employee's attire or the subtleties of navigating office dynamics, the details matter. "Enhancing Staff Performance: From Appearance to Interactions" seeks to unravel these details, offering a holistic approach to improving staff performance across an array of touchpoints.

The motivation behind this book stemmed from observing a gap in existing literature. While many books focus on individual aspects of professional development, few combine the intricacies of appearance, interpersonal relations, customer service, and hierarchical dynamics into a single, comprehensive guide.

Each chapter in this book is designed to be both theoretical and practical. We delve into the psychology and reasoning behind each topic, ensuring that readers not only know the 'what' but also the 'why'. This foundational understanding is then coupled with actionable advice, real-life scenarios, and templates that can be immediately implemented, bridging the gap between knowledge and application.

A noteworthy feature of this guide is its inclusivity. Recognizing that workplaces are becoming more diverse, both culturally and generationally, this book offers insights that cater to a broad audience. From the traditional corporate setting to the more relaxed startup culture, from Baby Boomers to Generation Z—there's something for everyone.

As you journey through the pages, you'll encounter a mix of expert opinions, case studies, and anecdotes from personal experiences. It is my hope that these stories will resonate, inspire, and perhaps even challenge some pre-existing notions.

"Enhancing Staff Performance" is not just for managers or HR professionals; it's for every individual who believes in the potential for continuous growth. Whether you're at the beginning of your career, finding your footing in a new role, or are a seasoned professional looking to refine certain skills, this book promises valuable insights.

In conclusion, the aim of this book is clear: to empower each reader to elevate their performance, foster healthier workplace relationships, and ultimately, contribute to the collective success of their organizations. Your journey towards enhanced performance begins now.

With gratitude and anticipation,

Dr. Salwa Elmeawad

Who Should Read This Book?

At a glance, "Enhancing Staff Performance: From Appearance to Interactions" might seem tailored exclusively for those in leadership or managerial roles. However, the principles, strategies, and insights contained within these pages hold value for a broad spectrum of readers. Here's a detailed breakdown of who should consider diving into this comprehensive guide:

1. **New Entrants to the Workforce**:

- **Why?** If you're a recent graduate or someone just starting out in your career, this book will offer a foundational understanding of workplace expectations, the significance of professional appearance, and the art of interpersonal interactions. It serves as a roadmap to navigating the complex dynamics of the professional realm.

2. **Experienced Professionals**:

- **Why?** Even seasoned professionals can benefit from revisiting and refining their interpersonal skills, understanding evolving workplace dynamics, and ensuring their appearance aligns with contemporary professional standards. This book offers advanced insights and nuanced techniques to further hone one's professional persona.

3. **Team Leaders and Managers**:

- **Why?** Leading a team requires more than just strategic thinking. Understanding how to cultivate a cohesive, high-performing team, mediate conflicts, and foster a culture of mutual respect is pivotal. This book equips leaders with the tools to not only enhance their own performance but to uplift their entire team.

4. **Human Resources Professionals**:

- **Why?** From drafting dress code policies to organizing training sessions and mediating conflicts, HR professionals play a pivotal role in shaping staff performance. This book provides a holistic approach to understanding and nurturing employee potential.

5. **Customer Service Representatives**:

- **Why?** With an entire chapter dedicated to mastering customer interactions, those in customer-facing roles will gain invaluable insights into handling diverse scenarios, managing difficult customers, and ensuring service excellence.

6. **Entrepreneurs and Small Business Owners**:

- **Why?** As you wear multiple hats, understanding every facet of employee performance becomes crucial. This book can guide you in setting the tone for your company culture, building strong intra-team relationships, and ensuring that customer interactions are top-notch.

7. **Consultants and Trainers**:

- **Why?** Those in the business of guiding other businesses can leverage the strategies, case studies, and practical advice in this book to enrich their training modules and consultation sessions.

8. **Students of Business and Management**:

- **Why?** As the leaders of tomorrow, gaining an early understanding of the intricacies of workplace dynamics, appearance, and interactions can set you apart. This book offers both theoretical knowledge and practical applications.

9. **Any Individual Passionate About Personal Development**:

- **Why?** If you believe in continuous growth, value effective communication, and aim to build fruitful relationships in and out of the workplace, this book will serve as a comprehensive resource.

In essence, "Enhancing Staff Performance: From Appearance to Interactions" is more than just a guide—it's an investment in one's professional journey. Whether you're directly involved in nurturing employee performance or simply looking to uplift your own, there's a wealth of knowledge waiting for you within these pages.

Disclaimer

While every effort has been made to ensure the accuracy and comprehensiveness of the information contained in "Enhancing Staff Performance: From Appearance to Interactions," readers are advised to use this book as a general guide and not as the ultimate source of subject matter expertise.

The content provided is based on the author's insights, research, and best understanding of the subjects discussed as of the publication date. However, practices, standards, and workplace dynamics can vary greatly across industries, cultures, and regions. Therefore, specific situations, environments, or changes that have occurred after the publication date may require different approaches or modifications to the strategies outlined in this book.

Neither the publisher nor the author shall be liable for any damages or losses of any kind, including direct, indirect, incidental, consequential, or punitive damages, arising out of or in connection with the use of this book or its content. This disclaimer includes, but is not limited to, errors or omissions in content, any interpretation or misinterpretation of information, or any action or decision taken by a reader based on the information provided.

It's essential for readers to consider their unique circumstances, consult with professionals where necessary, and exercise their judgment when implementing the advice or strategies discussed.

All case studies, examples, and anecdotes included in this book are provided for illustrative purposes and may be based on real events, hypothetical situations, or a combination thereof. Any resemblance to actual persons, living or dead, businesses, companies, events, or locales is purely coincidental unless explicitly stated otherwise.

The inclusion of external links, references, or citations does not imply endorsement of those sites or their content. The author and publisher are not responsible for the content of external sites or for any potential damage arising out of or in connection with the use or reliance on any such content.

All trademarks, service marks, and company names or logos mentioned in this book are the property of their respective owners and are used for identification purposes only. Use of these names, logos, and brands does not imply endorsement.

Happy reading!

Dr. Salwa ELmeawad

Table of Contents

Table of Contents

Chapter 1: Introduction

Staff performance, a concept that seemingly appears straightforward, is far from being just a measure of tasks completed or targets achieved. In the dynamic world of modern business, understanding what constitutes effective staff performance is crucial for both individuals and organizations. This vast landscape, evolving continuously with changes in work culture, technology, and societal values, influences organizational success, individual job satisfaction, and growth opportunities. The complexity and depth of staff performance warrant a comprehensive understanding.

1. Historical Evolution of Staff Performance

In the early 20th century, the industrial era's production-centric mindset primarily focused on the volume of output and efficiency (Taylor, 1911). The seminal work of Frederick Taylor on scientific management highlighted the importance of optimizing individual tasks for maximum productivity. This task-based evaluation gradually expanded its horizons as the service industry burgeoned, and the nature of work diversified.

Later, Drucker (1954) emphasized a shift from purely quantitative evaluations to more qualitative, holistic measures. In his understanding, the knowledge worker of the modern era required assessments based not only on 'how much' but also on 'how' and 'why' (Drucker, 1999). This paved the way for the multifaceted evaluations we see today.

2. Components of Staff Performance

Contemporary staff performance evaluation has evolved to recognize the multifarious roles an employee plays:

- **Task Performance**: Core job duties, like achieving sales targets or completing projects within deadlines (Borman & Motowidlo, 1993).

- **Contextual Performance**: Often overlooked, these are the contributions an employee makes outside of core tasks. This might include assisting colleagues, maintaining a positive work environment, or volunteering for extracurricular activities (Borman & Motowidlo, 1993).

- **Adaptive Performance**: Especially relevant in today's rapidly evolving workplaces, this refers to the ability of employees to adjust to changes – new technologies, shifting job roles, or unexpected challenges (Pulakos et al., 2000).

- **Counterproductive Work Behaviors**: These are negative actions that can harm an organization or its members, such as misconduct, theft, or withholding critical information (Sackett, 2002).

3. Performance Management: Beyond Evaluation

Evaluating staff performance isn't a standalone activity. It's part of an encompassing performance management process that includes:

- **Goal Setting**: Aligning individual goals with organizational objectives, often through SMART (Specific, Measurable, Achievable, Relevant, Time-bound) criteria (Doran, 1981).

- **Continuous Feedback**: Periodic check-ins and feedback mechanisms ensure alignment and address concerns before they escalate (London, 2003).

- **Formal Evaluations**: Annual or biannual reviews that assess achievements, challenges, and areas of improvement (DeNisi & Pritchard, 2006).

- **Development Plans**: Tailored plans to address skill gaps or prepare individuals for future roles (Noe, 2010).

4. The Imperative of Clarity and Fairness

An integral component of effective staff performance management is the perceived fairness and transparency of the process. When employees feel their performance evaluations are just, accurate, and devoid of bias, they are more likely to be engaged, motivated, and committed to their roles (Colquitt et al., 2001).

5. The Interplay of External Factors

External factors, including economic shifts, technological advancements, and societal values, influence performance expectations. For instance, the rise of remote work has shifted the emphasis from time-based evaluations to outcome-based assessments (Allen et al., 2015).

Conclusion

Understanding staff performance is not a mere exercise in evaluation but a deep dive into the intricate web of factors, behaviors, and outcomes that shape the modern workplace. As we delve deeper into this topic, this foundation will guide our exploration of strategies, challenges, and best practices.

The Factors Influencing Staff Performance:

The modern professional landscape is a complex web of variables, and within this intricate framework, staff performance emerges

Chapter 1: Introduction

as both a crucial metric and a multifaceted phenomenon. An organization's vitality and success are inexorably linked to the performance of its staff. Yet, what exactly influences this performance? It's an amalgamation of intrinsic motivators, external pressures, personal dynamics, and overarching organizational structures.

Understanding the myriad areas that impact staff performance is paramount, not only for organizational leadership aiming to cultivate excellence but also for individuals seeking personal growth and professional advancement. This exploration into the determinants of staff performance will shed light on the intrinsic and extrinsic factors that shape individual contributions within an organizational setting.

1. Intrinsic Motivation

At the heart of any discussion about performance lies the concept of intrinsic motivation. Deci and Ryan's (1985) Self-Determination Theory posits that individuals are most motivated when they feel autonomous and that their work is aligned with their personal values and interests. This internal drive often surpasses external motivators and can lead to higher job satisfaction and, by extension, better performance (Ryan & Deci, 2000).

2. Training and Development Opportunities

Training and development are pivotal. Staff equipped with the requisite knowledge and skills can navigate their roles effectively (Noe, 2010). Continuous learning opportunities also signal organizational investment in employees, which can boost morale and performance (Aguinis & Kraiger, 2009).

3. Feedback Mechanisms

Regular, constructive feedback provides employees with a clear understanding of their strengths and areas for improvement (London, 2003). Effective feedback can catalyze personal growth and lead to enhanced performance (DeNisi & Kluger, 2000).

4. Work Environment and Organizational Culture

An organization's culture and the immediate work environment substantially influence staff morale and performance. Aspects like open communication, respect, inclusivity, and a sense of belonging can foster a positive work environment and enhance performance (Denison, 1990).

5. Work-Life Balance

With the blurring boundaries of work, especially in the digital era, achieving a harmonious work-life balance is challenging. Overwork and burnout can drastically affect performance, making balance essential for sustained high performance (Greenhaus & Beutell, 1985).

6. Leadership and Management Styles

Leaders play a pivotal role in shaping team performance. Leadership styles, be it transformational, transactional, or laissez-faire, influence staff motivation, commitment, and overall output (Bass, 1999).

7. Team Dynamics and Interpersonal Relationships

Positive interpersonal relationships and effective team dynamics can enhance collective and individual performance. Trust, open communication, and mutual respect within teams contribute significantly to overall productivity (Tuckman, 1965).

8. Compensation and Rewards

Chapter 1: Introduction

While intrinsic motivation is paramount, extrinsic motivators, such as competitive compensation, benefits, and rewards, cannot be overlooked. Fair compensation and acknowledgment can boost morale and drive performance (Lawler, 1971).

9. Tools, Technology, and Infrastructure

The importance of providing staff with the right tools and technology is often underestimated. Efficient systems and supportive infrastructure can streamline processes, reduce frustration, and enhance performance (Goodhue & Thompson, 1995).

10. Personal Factors and Individual Differences

Personal life events, health, individual personality traits, and even daily mood fluctuations can impact job performance. Recognizing and accommodating these personal factors can make a significant difference in understanding and enhancing staff performance (Barrick & Mount, 1991).

Conclusion

The tapestry of staff performance is woven with threads from various domains – psychological, environmental, organizational, personal, and more. By understanding and navigating these multifaceted influences, organizations can cultivate environments that not only foster excellence but also nurture the holistic well-being of their staff.

The Imperative of Developing Staff Performance:

In the intricate tapestry of organizational success, one thread consistently stands out as pivotal: the performance of its staff. It is not merely about achieving targets but encompasses the holistic development of individuals to drive collective growth. This introductory exploration delves into the profound significance of developing staff performance, its implications on individuals, teams, and organizations, and the ripple effects on the broader economic and social landscape.

1. The Organizational Imperative

The quality of staff performance can make or break an organization. A McKinsey report (Bryan & Joyce, 2005) postulated that a high-performing team could be 20% more productive than an average team. But what truly makes this figure resonate is the compound effect it has over time, drastically impacting organizational growth, profitability, and market position.

2. The Link to Job Satisfaction

Well-developed staff performance is often correlated with higher job satisfaction. When individuals are trained, guided, and equipped to perform at their best, it instills a sense of accomplishment and purpose, which in turn enhances job satisfaction (Judge et al., 2001).

3. Economic Implications

On a macro scale, developing staff performance has profound implications on the economy. A well-performing workforce drives organizational growth, which leads to increased hiring, more investments, and eventually, positive economic growth (Combs et al., 2006).

4. Staff Retention and Organizational Loyalty

Chapter 1: Introduction

Continuous development and performance management have been shown to foster staff loyalty and reduce turnover rates. The costs associated with employee turnover - both tangible and intangible - are significant, making staff performance development not just a matter of growth but also of retention (Hausknecht et al., 2009).

5. The Role in Innovation

Innovation is the lifeblood of the modern business landscape. A workforce that is continuously developed is better positioned to innovate, adapt to changing market dynamics, and drive an organization forward in novel directions (Gupta & Singhal, 1993).

6. Enhancing Customer Satisfaction

A direct offshoot of enhanced staff performance is improved customer satisfaction. Well-trained and high-performing staff can address customer needs more effectively, fostering loyalty and enhancing brand reputation (Harter et al., 2002).

7. Personal Growth and Career Development

Developing staff performance isn't just about the organization. On an individual level, it translates to personal growth, skill acquisition, and career advancement opportunities. It prepares employees for future leadership roles and equips them with a versatile skill set (London, 1983).

8. The Societal Ripple Effect

A well-developed workforce creates ripples in the broader societal framework. Employees with higher job satisfaction, growth opportunities, and performance levels contribute more positively to society, both economically and culturally (Greenhaus et al., 2003).

9. Future Preparedness

In an era characterized by rapid technological advancements and unpredictable market shifts, developing staff performance is about future-proofing an organization. It ensures adaptability, resilience, and the ability to pivot effectively in the face of unforeseen challenges (Schwartz & McCarthy, 2007).

The magnitude of developing staff performance cannot be overstated. It's a symbiotic relationship where both the organization and its employees benefit, creating a positive feedback loop of growth, satisfaction, and success. As we delve deeper into the nuances of this subject, it becomes evident that staff performance development is not just a good-to-have but an absolute imperative in the contemporary professional landscape.

Key Areas of Focus in Staff Performance:

Staff performance, while central to the organizational fabric, is not a singular, isolated construct. It is a nuanced, multi-dimensional phenomenon shaped by a plethora of factors. For businesses and professionals seeking to maximize this performance, it is vital to have a clear overview of the pivotal areas of focus. These areas not only guide the strategies and interventions employed but also shape the trajectory of individual and collective growth. In this comprehensive introduction, we'll embark on an exploration of these key areas, shedding light on their relevance, interplay, and overarching impact on the realm of staff performance.

1. Personal Motivation and Engagement

At the foundation of staff performance lies the personal motivation of the individual. According to Ryan and Deci's Self-Determination Theory (2000), intrinsic motivation, autonomy, competence, and relatedness significantly influence an individual's enthusiasm and commitment to their role. Engaged employees are not only more productive but also contribute positively to team dynamics and overall organizational culture.

2. Skill Development and Training

In a constantly evolving business landscape, the significance of continuous skill development cannot be overstated. Training programs, workshops, and seminars play a pivotal role in equipping staff with the necessary tools to navigate their roles effectively (Noe, 2010). Moreover, they foster adaptability, ensuring that employees remain relevant in changing industry scenarios.

3. Feedback and Communication

Regular, transparent communication is the linchpin of effective staff performance management. Constructive feedback, both positive and developmental, provides individuals with a clear roadmap of their strengths and areas of improvement, promoting a culture of continuous growth (London, 2003).

4. Goal Setting and Alignment

Clearly defined goals, aligned with broader organizational objectives, offer direction and purpose. The SMART (Specific, Measurable, Achievable, Relevant, Time-bound) framework provides a structured approach to goal-setting, ensuring that staff have clear, tangible targets to work towards (Doran, 1981).

5. Organizational Culture and Environment

The environment in which individuals operate plays a critical role in shaping their performance. A positive organizational culture, characterized by mutual respect, open communication, and a shared vision, can significantly boost staff morale and productivity (Denison, 1990).

6. Work-Life Balance

In today's fast-paced world, the importance of work-life balance is paramount. Overwork and burnout can severely impede performance. Organizations that recognize and promote a harmonious balance between professional and personal lives witness higher job satisfaction and reduced turnover (Greenhaus & Beutell, 1985).

7. Leadership and Supervision

The role of leadership in shaping staff performance is monumental. Leaders who inspire, guide, and support their teams foster an environment of trust, motivation, and high performance. Transformational leadership, in particular, has been linked to increased staff motivation and superior team outcomes (Bass, 1999).

8. Tools, Technology, and Infrastructure

In the digital age, equipping staff with the right tools and technologies is essential. Efficient systems can significantly streamline processes, reduce redundancies, and enhance overall staff performance (Goodhue & Thompson, 1995).

9. Compensation, Benefits, and Incentives

While intrinsic motivation is a significant driver, extrinsic rewards such as competitive compensation, benefits, and performance-based incentives also play a role in shaping staff performance. Fair and equitable compensation can boost morale, commitment, and drive (Lawler, 1971).

10. Team Dynamics and Collaboration

The dynamics within a team and the collaboration between different teams can significantly influence individual performance. Trust, mutual respect, and effective communication within teams lead to synergy, where the collective output exceeds the sum of individual contributions (Tuckman, 1965).

Conclusion

Navigating the multifaceted world of staff performance requires a clear understanding of these key areas of focus. Each area, while distinct, is interconnected, and their collective influence shapes the trajectory of individual and organizational success. As we delve deeper into each domain in the subsequent chapters, the importance of a holistic, integrated approach to staff performance becomes increasingly evident.

Chapter 2: The Significance of Dress Codes at Work

In the intricate landscape of professional culture, certain elements subtly yet powerfully shape perceptions, behaviors, and the overall ethos of the workplace. One such element, often overlooked yet deeply influential, is the dress code. What we wear to work isn't merely about personal expression or fashion but reflects broader themes of professionalism, organizational identity, inclusivity, and psychological well-being. This comprehensive introduction seeks to unravel the many facets of dress codes at work, shedding light on its significance in shaping both individual and collective narratives in the professional realm.

1. Historical Context of Workplace Attire:

Historically, workplace attire has evolved in tandem with socio-cultural norms and economic shifts. From the strictly tailored suits of the 1950s corporate world to the tech start-up casuals of the 2000s, workplace attire is a reflection of societal values and the nature of work (Entwistle, 2000). Each era brings forth its unique style, and with it, implicit messages about power, status, and identity.

The clothing we wear to work has always been a reflection of broader societal contexts. As societies and their economic foundations evolved, so too did the dress codes within their workplaces. Delving deeper into the historical transformations of workplace attire can provide invaluable insights into the cultural, economic, and technological shifts of their times.

A. Industrial Revolution and Uniformity (Late 18th to Early 20th Century)

Chapter 2: The Significance of Dress Codes at Work

The onset of the Industrial Revolution brought about significant changes in workplace attire. Factories and industrial establishments often mandated uniforms for practicality and safety. These uniforms also created a sense of unity and equality among workers, but at the expense of individual expression. Simultaneously, managerial and administrative roles started to emphasize the importance of suits, ties, and formal wear, symbolizing authority and professionalism (Hollander, 1994).

B. The Corporate Boom of the Mid-20th Century

Post World War II, with the corporate boom and the rise of white-collar jobs, the suit became the quintessential attire for men in the workplace. For women, entering the workforce in larger numbers than ever before, the 1950s and 60s were characterized by tailored dresses, skirts, and modest blouses. This era epitomized formality and underscored the values of conformity, professionalism, and hierarchy (Craik, 2005).

C. The Cultural Revolution of the 1960s and 70s

The late 1960s and early 70s, marked by socio-cultural upheavals, saw a challenge to conventional norms across society, including workplace attire. The hippie movement, the rise of youth culture, and the feminist movement all influenced the gradual relaxation of strict dress codes. Colorful shirts, flared pants, and less formal attire began making their way into the workplace (Tseëlon, 2001).

D. The Tech Revolution and Casual Fridays (Late 20th Century)

By the 1990s, with the rapid growth of Silicon Valley and the tech industry, workplace attire underwent another transformation. Tech giants like Steve Jobs and Mark Zuckerberg popularized casual wear, signaling a shift from traditional corporate values. Additionally, the introduction of 'Casual Fridays' became a widespread phenomenon, offering a break from the monotony of formal wear and reflecting a blend of work and leisure (Roach-Higgins & Eicher, 1992).

E. The 21st Century: Personalization and Remote Work

The 21st century has seen a further democratization of workplace attire. With the gig economy, freelancing, and remote work on the rise, there's been a noticeable shift towards comfort and personal expression. Moreover, the COVID-19 pandemic and the consequent rise of work-from-home models have blurred the lines between professional and casual wear, with many questioning the future relevance of strict dress codes (Peluchette & Karl, 2007).

The transformation of workplace attire through the ages is a testament to its deep-seated connection with socio-cultural and economic shifts. It's more than just fabric and fashion; it's a narrative of changing values, economic structures, and societal norms.

2. Dress Codes as a Reflection of Organizational Culture:

A company's dress code can provide a glimpse into its organizational culture and values (Rafaeli & Pratt, 1993). While some organizations advocate formal attire to emphasize hierarchy, precision, and formality, others might promote casual wear, reflecting values of flexibility, creativity, and egalitarianism.

The saying "clothes make the man" holds considerable weight in professional settings. The attire individuals adorn, especially in workplaces, can reveal more than personal style; it provides a window into the organization's culture, values, and ethos. While attire is just one piece of the organizational culture puzzle, its significance in shaping and reflecting workplace norms, hierarchies, and values cannot be understated. Delving deeper into this aspect offers a nuanced understanding of the intricate relationship between dress codes and organizational culture.

A. Signifier of Professionalism and Standards

For many traditional corporations, especially in sectors such as finance, law, and consultancy, formal dress codes—such as suits, ties, and dress shoes—are more than a mere tradition. They signify a commitment to excellence, professionalism, and high standards. These attire norms subtly communicate the organization's seriousness about its work, its respect for clients, and the value it places on attention to detail (Rafaeli & Pratt, 1993).

B. Expressing Organizational Identity

Companies often use dress codes as an extension of their branding strategy. Take, for instance, tech giants like Apple or companies like Virgin Atlantic. Their employee attire, whether it's the casual simplicity of a black turtleneck or the iconic red uniforms of flight attendants, becomes synonymous with the brand itself, reflecting organizational identity and ethos (Schroeder, 2005).

C. Egalitarianism vs. Hierarchy

Organizations that promote a flat structure or value egalitarianism might encourage casual or flexible dress codes. This approach can blur the visual distinctions between different levels of the organization, fostering a sense of equality and camaraderie (Chen et al., 2015). In contrast, firms with a more hierarchical structure may have distinct dress norms for different tiers, emphasizing rank and authority.

D. Fostering Creativity and Individualism

Industries that value creativity, like advertising or fashion, often have relaxed or open-ended dress codes. Such freedom in attire choice can spur creativity, allowing employees to express their individuality and feel unrestricted, which in turn might boost innovation and out-of-the-box thinking (Kwon & Parham, 1994).

E. Inclusivity and Respect for Diversity

Modern organizations are increasingly recognizing the importance of diversity and inclusion. This shift is reflected in more inclusive dress codes that accommodate different cultural, religious, and personal preferences. Such dress codes send a powerful message about the organization's values and its commitment to creating a welcoming environment for everyone (Syed & Özbilgin, 2009).

F. Reflecting Work Nature and Practicality

In certain industries, dress codes are determined primarily by the nature of the job. For instance, healthcare professionals, construction workers, or laboratory researchers wear attire that prioritizes safety and functionality. Such dress codes reflect the organization's commitment to employee safety and the practical demands of the job (Joseph & Alex, 1972).

Dress codes, in their myriad forms, serve as silent communicators of an organization's culture, values, and priorities. While they might seem superficial at first glance, they play a pivotal role in shaping internal dynamics, external perceptions, and the overall ethos of a workplace.

3. First Impressions and Professional Perception:

Clothing profoundly influences first impressions. Research suggests that within seconds of meeting someone, judgments about professionalism, trustworthiness, and competence are made, largely based on attire (Kwintessential, 2010). A well-thought-out dress code can thus set the tone for interactions both within and outside the organization.

The significance of first impressions in professional settings cannot be overstated. Often, before a word is spoken or a handshake exchanged, judgments have already been made. The attire one wears acts as an immediate, non-verbal communicator, setting the tone for subsequent interactions and shaping perceptions of professionalism, competence, and fit. A deeper exploration into the role of workplace attire in influencing first impressions and professional perceptions reveals the profound implications of sartorial choices on individual and organizational success.

A. The Power of the First Glimpse

Studies have consistently shown that human beings form impressions in mere seconds. Willis and Todorov (2006) found that individuals make trait inferences about others after viewing their faces for only 100 milliseconds. Extend this to attire, and it becomes clear that clothing choices play a pivotal role in shaping these rapid judgments. While such snap judgments may seem superficial, they can have lasting implications for interactions, evaluations, and decision-making processes.

B. Attire and Perceived Competence

A person's choice of clothing can deeply influence perceptions of their competence. Kraus and Mendes (2014) conducted studies demonstrating that individuals wearing formal clothing were perceived as more competent than those in casual attire. Furthermore, those dressed more formally were also attributed higher levels of status and perceived to hold more significant positions within an organization.

C. Credibility and Trustworthiness

Trustworthiness is a cornerstone of professional interactions. Clothing can serve as a visual cue signaling reliability and credibility. A study by Howlett et al. (2013) suggested that attire could influence perceptions of a person's trustworthiness, with formal attire generally being associated with higher levels of credibility, particularly in professions such as law or finance.

D. Conformity vs. Individuality

While dressing according to established norms can signify professionalism and commitment, showcasing individuality through attire can also be advantageous. Depending on the organizational culture, unique sartorial choices can signal creativity, independence, and a break from the status quo (Belk, 1988). However, this balance between conformity and individuality is delicate and should align with the expectations and values of the workplace.

E. Influence on Self-Perception

Interestingly, attire doesn't just influence how others perceive an individual, but it also affects how individuals perceive themselves. The concept of "enclothed cognition," posited by Adam and Galinsky (2012), suggests that the symbolic meaning of clothing and the sensory experience of wearing it can influence the wearer's cognitive processes and performance.

F. The Role in Non-verbal Communication

In addition to verbal cues, non-verbal communication plays a crucial role in interpersonal interactions. Clothing is a form of non-verbal communication, conveying information about an individual's background, personality, status, and role. As Mehrabian (1972) noted, in situations where verbal and non-verbal messages conflict, people tend to trust the non-verbal more.

First impressions, shaped significantly by attire, play a pivotal role in the realm of professional interactions. As organizations and professionals navigate the intricate web of workplace dynamics, understanding the profound influence of sartorial choices becomes paramount. Dressing not only for the role one has but for the role one aspires to can set the trajectory for professional growth and success.

4. Dress Codes and Employee Productivity:

What we wear can influence our cognitive processes and behaviors. For instance, findings from a study by Adam & Galinsky (2012) indicated that certain clothing items could boost attention, alertness, and even performance on specific tasks. Hence, dress codes might play an unforeseen role in shaping employee productivity.

Dress codes, whether explicitly stated or implicitly understood, permeate the professional realm. Beyond the clear demarcation of professional standards or the reinforcement of company brand and culture, the attire employees don holds significant sway over their productivity levels. As we delve deeper into this relationship, the multifaceted impact of sartorial choices on individual work output, cognitive processes, and overall workplace efficiency becomes evident.

A. Enclothed Cognition and Cognitive Processes

"Enclothed cognition" is a term coined to describe the systematic influence that clothes have on the wearer's psychological processes. A study by Adam and Galinsky (2012) demonstrated that wearing specific types of attire could change the wearer's psychological state. For instance, participants wearing lab coats displayed heightened attention compared to those not wearing them. Such findings suggest that workplace attire can directly influence cognitive functions crucial for productivity.

B. Dress Codes and Task Performance

The nature of attire can influence how employees approach and perform specific tasks. For instance, formal attire has been associated with enhanced abstract thinking, facilitating broader organizational vision and strategic planning (Slepian et al., 2015). In contrast, casual wear might encourage comfort, potentially boosting creativity and out-of-the-box thinking—essential for roles demanding innovation.

C. Psychological Comfort and Well-being

Feeling comfortable in one's attire is intrinsically linked with mental well-being. A restrictive or inappropriate dress code might result in discomfort, reducing an individual's focus and hampering productivity. On the flip side, attire that aligns with an individual's personal comfort can enhance self-confidence, indirectly boosting productivity (Peluchette & Karl, 2007).

D. Role Suitability and Professional Alignment

The alignment of attire with professional roles is essential. For instance, customer-facing roles in sectors like banking or consultancy might necessitate formal attire, underscoring professionalism and trust. On the other hand, creative roles in advertising or design agencies might benefit from a more relaxed dress code, reflecting the industry's creative and fluid nature (Rafaeli et al., 1997).

E. Impact on Interpersonal Interactions

Employee productivity isn't solely based on individual tasks but is also influenced by interpersonal interactions. Attire plays a role in these dynamics. Proper dress codes can level the playing field, reducing potential biases and ensuring that interactions are based on merit rather than appearance-based judgments (Kawamura, 2005).

F. Conformity, Autonomy, and Decision Fatigue

While dress codes ensure uniformity, they also reduce the daily decision-making burden regarding attire—a phenomenon related to decision fatigue. By reducing trivial decisions about clothing, employees can channel their cognitive resources towards more critical tasks (Vohs et al., 2008).

Dress codes, while seemingly a matter of aesthetics, hold substantial implications for employee productivity. Organizations aiming to optimize productivity must consider the nuanced relationship between attire and performance, ensuring that dress codes resonate with the nature of work, employee well-being, and overall organizational goals.

5. The Psychological Impacts of Dress:

Dress codes can have a profound psychological impact on employees. Wearing formal attire has been linked to enhanced abstract thinking and big-picture processing (Slepian et al., 2015). On the contrary, casual attire can foster a sense of comfort, authenticity, and ease.

Attire extends beyond the fabric we drape on our bodies; it wields the power to influence our psyche in multifaceted ways. The clothes we wear can shape our mood, self-perception, cognitive abilities, and interactions with others. By diving deeper into the psychological impacts of dress, we come to understand its profound influence on individual identity, self-efficacy, and overall mental well-being in professional settings.

A. Enclothed Cognition and Psychological States

The term "enclothed cognition" encapsulates the concept that the clothes we wear can influence our psychological states. Adam and Galinsky (2012) demonstrated that wearing specific types of clothing, like a lab coat, could enhance attention and focus. This suggests that our attire can imbue us with certain characteristics or qualities associated with that particular clothing item.

B. Dress and Self-Perception

Our clothing choices are intertwined with our self-perception and self-worth. For many, dressing well or in alignment with professional standards can bolster self-confidence and feelings of competence. This phenomenon is supported by the Symbolic Interactionism theory, which posits that individuals derive meaning and identity from their interactions and the symbols in their environment, including clothing (Blumer, 1969).

C. Mood Regulation and Clothing

Clothing can serve as a tool for mood regulation. A study by Pine (2014) found that specific clothing could uplift spirits during challenging times. For instance, wearing bright colors or favorite outfits might elevate mood, providing an emotional boost that could be particularly beneficial in stressful professional scenarios.

D. Attire as a Social Facilitator

In social and professional settings, attire can act as an icebreaker or a conversation starter. Clothing that reflects personal interests or cultural backgrounds can foster connections and mutual understanding, enhancing interpersonal dynamics in the workplace (Rafaeli & Pratt, 1993).

E. The Double-Edged Sword of Conformity

While dressing in line with organizational norms can instill a sense of belonging and reduce feelings of alienation, it can also stifle individual expression. The tension between personal expression and organizational conformity can influence psychological well-being, especially for those who value individuality (Ibarra, 1999).

F. Cultural and Identity Affirmation

For many, clothing is an expression of cultural or personal identity. In multicultural workplaces, attire can be a way of holding onto cultural roots and asserting one's unique identity. This cultural expression can foster a sense of pride and grounding, reinforcing psychological well-being (Syed & Özbilgin, 2009).

G. Impact of Restrictiveness and Comfort

Wearing restrictive or uncomfortable clothing can have tangible psychological effects. Discomfort can be a distraction, reducing focus and cognitive capabilities. Furthermore, feeling physically restricted might even translate to feelings of psychological restriction, impinging on creativity and holistic well-being (Peluchette & Karl, 2007).

The intricate dance between attire and psychology showcases the profound impact of our sartorial choices. As individuals and organizations navigate the world of professional attire, understanding its psychological implications is paramount. Whether it's fostering a sense of belonging, asserting individuality, or simply elevating mood, the clothes we wear hold power over our psychological landscapes.

6. The Nuances of Inclusivity:

In our diverse globalized world, dress codes tread the fine line between standardization and inclusivity. An inclusive dress code recognizes and respects cultural, religious, and personal differences while fostering a sense of belonging (Syed & Özbilgin, 2009).

The globalized world, with its diverse cultures, religions, and lifestyles, mandates a fresh look at dress codes, especially in professional settings. Gone are the days when one-size-fits-all policies could be applied without a second thought. Today, dress codes intersect with inclusivity, reflecting an organization's commitment to honoring and valuing diversity. By delving deeper into the nuances of inclusivity in dress codes, we can appreciate the critical balance between maintaining organizational identity and respecting individual differences.

Chapter 2: The Significance of Dress Codes at Work

A. Cultural Sensitivity and Recognition

Across the globe, attire is steeped in cultural symbolism and significance. From the Indian saree to the Japanese kimono, traditional outfits are embodiments of cultural heritage and pride. Organizations, by recognizing and allowing such attire, send a strong signal of cultural sensitivity and inclusivity (Syed & Kramar, 2010).

B. Accommodating Religious Practices

For many, clothing isn't just about personal or cultural choice but is also deeply tied to religious beliefs. Whether it's the hijab in Islam, the turban in Sikhism, or the yarmulke in Judaism, these pieces of attire hold religious significance. Inclusive dress codes accommodate such religious wear, ensuring that individuals don't have to choose between their faith and their profession (Rippin, 2012).

C. Gender Identity and Expression

Inclusivity in dress codes extends to recognizing and respecting diverse gender identities. By moving away from strictly binary dress codes and allowing employees the flexibility to dress in a manner that aligns with their gender identity, organizations create a supportive environment for transgender, non-binary, and gender-nonconforming individuals (Johnson & Ng, 2016).

D. Physical Abilities and Comfort

Inclusive dress codes also cater to those with physical disabilities or medical needs. For instance, individuals who use prosthetics or wheelchairs might have specific clothing needs. An inclusive dress code takes these considerations into account, emphasizing comfort and functionality without compromising on professionalism (Stone & Colella, 1996).

E. The Mental Health Angle

Strict or inflexible dress codes can lead to anxiety and discomfort for some individuals. Inclusivity means recognizing such mental health implications and offering flexibility where needed. This might mean allowing more casual attire for those with anxiety disorders or creating safe spaces where individuals can discuss any dress-related concerns (Avey et al., 2010).

F. Balancing Inclusivity with Organizational Identity

While inclusivity is paramount, organizations also need to maintain a cohesive identity. This balance requires thoughtful policies that honor individual differences while ensuring that the organization presents a united front, especially in client-facing roles or public events (Ravazzani, 2016).

Inclusivity in dress codes isn't merely a matter of ticking off checkboxes in the diversity and inclusion agenda. It's about creating a workplace where every individual feels seen, respected, and valued. When dress codes are crafted with empathy and understanding, they become powerful tools that reinforce an organization's commitment to a diverse, inclusive, and harmonious workplace.

7. Dress Codes in the Age of Remote Work:

The rise of remote work has brought forth new questions about dress codes. How does one navigate professionalism in the digital realm? And does dressing up for work, even if unseen, still matter? The blurring lines between personal and professional spaces provide an interesting dimension to the discourse on dress codes (Bailey & Kurland, 2002).

The rise of remote work has fundamentally altered many aspects of traditional professional norms, including dress codes. The boundaries of professional attire have been redefined as employees transition from corporate boardrooms to Zoom meetings from their living rooms. Navigating this new terrain requires an understanding of the psychological, functional, and organizational implications of dress in a remote work setting. Let's delve deeper into how dress codes have evolved in the age of remote work and the nuances accompanying this shift.

A. The Psychological Continuity of Dressing for Work

Despite the shift to remote work, the psychological benefits of dressing for the job persist. Research suggests that our attire can influence our mental state, productivity, and work performance. For instance, a study by Adam and Galinsky (2012) proposed the concept of "enclothed cognition," where wearing specific attire (like a formal shirt or even just work shoes) can invoke feelings of professionalism and enhance focus, even in a remote setting.

B. The Shift to 'Camera-Ready' Attire

The rise of video conferencing tools like Zoom and Microsoft Teams has given birth to a new dress code dynamic: being 'camera-ready.' This often means professionals might dress formally from the waist up while opting for comfort from the waist down. The emphasis is on presenting a polished image in the frame, even if it's paired with pajama bottoms or athletic shorts out of view (Wiederhold, 2020).

C. Emphasizing Comfort and Functionality

One of the evident shifts in remote work attire is the increased emphasis on comfort. With no commute and a home setting, many have gravitated towards more comfortable attire like loungewear, activewear, or even relaxed-fit clothing. This trend aligns with the broader movement towards valuing employee well-being and mental health (Petrilli et al., 2020).

D. Reflecting Personal and Organizational Brand

While remote work offers more flexibility in dress, it's essential for employees to consider how their attire reflects their personal and organizational brand. This is especially crucial for client-facing roles, where impressions still matter, even in a virtual environment. Personal branding, in this sense, is intertwined with attire choices and can influence perceptions of credibility and professionalism (Labrecque et al., 2011).

E. Cultural and Inclusivity Considerations

Remote work, by breaking geographical boundaries, has led to increasingly diverse teams spread across different countries and cultures. Dress codes in such a setting must be sensitive to various cultural norms, traditions, and practices. What's deemed appropriate in one culture might be different in another, necessitating a flexible and inclusive approach to dress codes (Glaveanu et al., 2019).

F. Future of Dress Codes in Hybrid Work Models

As organizations explore hybrid work models, combining in-office days with remote work, there's a need to establish clear and flexible dress code guidelines. These guidelines must bridge the gap between traditional office attire and the relaxed norms of remote work, offering clarity and consistency for employees (Kniffin et al., 2021).

The evolution of dress codes in the age of remote work reflects broader shifts in work cultures, values, and norms. As the lines between work and home blur, organizations and employees alike must navigate the nuanced dynamics of attire, balancing professionalism with comfort, and tradition with flexibility.

8. The Challenges and Critiques:

While dress codes carry numerous benefits, they aren't without challenges and critiques. Issues of enforcement, perceived restrictiveness, or potential bias require thoughtful consideration (Peluchette & Karl, 2007).

As remote work reshapes professional environments, dress codes too have come under scrutiny. While some organizations have adapted and evolved their dress guidelines, others grapple with the challenges posed by this new paradigm. The critiques associated with dress codes in remote work contexts range from their relevance and enforceability to deeper issues of equity and inclusion. Let's explore these challenges and critiques in greater detail.

A. Relevance and Necessity

The most fundamental critique is the very relevance of dress codes in a remote work setting. Critics argue that as long as the work is completed efficiently, the attire an employee chooses in the comfort of their home shouldn't matter. The emphasis, they suggest, should be on output and results rather than appearance (Bailey & Kurland, 2002).

B. Enforceability and Surveillance

Even if an organization wishes to uphold a specific dress code, the enforceability of such policies in a remote setting is challenging. Enforcing dress codes might necessitate intrusive surveillance measures, raising concerns about employee privacy and autonomy (Zuboff, 2019).

C. Potential for Bias and Discrimination

Dress codes, if not thoughtfully implemented, can inadvertently perpetuate biases. In a remote setting, these biases can become even more pronounced. For instance, employees from diverse cultural or socio-economic backgrounds might not have the means or the cultural inclination to adhere to Western-centric professional attire norms, leading to inadvertent discrimination (Syed & Kramar, 2010).

D. The Economic Burden on Employees

Expecting employees to maintain a certain dress standard for virtual meetings or video calls can impose an economic burden. Not everyone might have the financial means to invest in "camera-ready" attire, especially when the majority of their workdays are spent off-camera (Hilbrecht et al., 2008).

E. The Mental and Emotional Strain

Dress codes in remote work can add an additional layer of mental and emotional strain for employees. The expectation to "dress up" can create stress, detracting from the comfort advantages that remote work is supposed to offer (Mann & Holdsworth, 2003).

F. Overemphasis on Appearance Over Substance

A stringent focus on dress codes can inadvertently shift the focus from substance to appearance. There's a risk that too much emphasis on how employees appear in virtual meetings detracts from the content and quality of their contributions (Nippert-Eng, 1996).

G. Dress Codes and Gender Dynamics

Gender dynamics play a significant role in dress code critiques. Historically, women have been subjected to more rigorous scrutiny regarding professional attire. In remote work settings, there's a risk of these gendered expectations persisting, with women feeling pressured to adhere to certain beauty standards on camera (Wajcman, 1998).

While dress codes have traditionally been seen as a way to maintain professionalism and cohesion, their application in the age of remote work is fraught with challenges. Organizations must tread carefully, ensuring that their policies promote inclusivity, equity, and respect for individual autonomy.

Conclusion

The significance of dress codes at work extends far beyond fabric and fashion. It delves deep into the realms of identity, psychology, culture, and organizational ethos. As we further explore this topic, the multifaceted impacts and profound implications of what we wear to work become increasingly evident.

Discuss the psychology behind attire and first impressions:

The age-old adage, "Don't judge a book by its cover," often serves as a cautionary note against the pitfalls of superficial judgments. However, in the complex tapestry of human interactions, the reality is that covers—or in this case, attire—often play a defining role in shaping perceptions. Before we speak, our clothes have already whispered tales about our background, personality, status, and even intentions. Understanding the underlying psychology of how attire molds first impressions is pivotal, especially in contexts where these initial judgments can set the tone for future interactions. In this introduction, we'll traverse the intricate pathways linking attire, psychology, and first impressions.

1. Evolutionary Roots of Judgments

At the heart of our instinct to judge based on appearances are evolutionary underpinnings. Historically, rapid assessments of potential threats or allies, based on minimal cues, could mean the difference between survival and peril. While we've evolved considerably, our brains remain wired for quick categorizations—a mechanism referred to as 'thin slicing' by Ambady and Rosenthal (1992). They demonstrated that people could make accurate assessments about others in mere seconds, or even less.

2. Clothing as Non-verbal Communication

Much of human communication is non-verbal. Mehrabian (1972) noted that in certain situations, non-verbal cues could carry more weight than the actual words spoken. Attire is a significant component of this non-verbal matrix. Through our clothing choices, we consciously or unconsciously convey messages about our identity, status, mood, and more.

3. The Primacy and Recency Effects

The primacy effect, a cognitive bias, causes us to better recall the first items in a list or the initial moments in an interaction. The attire, in any meeting or interaction, benefits from this primacy effect. It's among the first things noticed, and thus, its impact on the impression is magnified (Murphy et al., 1985).

4. Attire, Stereotypes, and Expectancy Violations

Clothing often activates societal stereotypes, whether related to professionalism, socio-economic status, or cultural backgrounds. When attire aligns with a stereotype, it reinforces the initial impression. However, when it violates the expectation—like an entrepreneur in casual jeans and a t-shirt at a formal business meeting—it can lead to more intense scrutiny, a phenomenon explored in expectancy violations theory (Burgoon, 1993).

5. Symbolic Interactions and Attire

Blumer (1969) proposed symbolic interactionism, emphasizing that individuals ascribe meanings to objects, events, and behaviors based on the symbolic value they hold. Clothing, laden with symbolic meanings—whether a power suit or a wedding dress—elicits reactions and judgments rooted in these symbolic associations.

6. The Halo Effect and Clothing

The halo effect, as articulated by Nisbett and Wilson (1977), is a cognitive bias where our impression of someone in one domain influences our judgment of them in other unrelated domains. For instance, someone dressed sharply might be perceived as more competent, even without any evidence of their actual abilities.

7. Self-perception and Attire

Interestingly, attire doesn't just shape how others perceive us, but it also molds our self-perception. The concept of "enclothed cognition," proposed by Adam and Galinsky (2012), suggests that clothes can influence the wearer's cognitive processes. Wearing formal attire might imbue feelings of power and competence, while comfortable clothes might evoke relaxation.

Conclusion

The confluence of attire and first impressions resides at the intersection of psychology, sociology, and personal aesthetics. In a world increasingly driven by visual imagery—be it in person or digital—understanding the undercurrents shaping these judgments becomes crucial. Whether leveraging this knowledge for personal or professional reasons, the undeniable truth remains: attire, often silent, speaks volumes.

Highlight how appearance plays a role in brand representation:

In today's visual-centric world, appearance isn't merely a superficial attribute; it's a powerful narrative tool. Businesses and individuals alike have come to recognize that how they present themselves—both physically and virtually—serves as an embodiment of their brand's ethos, values, and promises. Just as a person's attire can communicate volumes about their personality and preferences, a brand's visual representation provides critical clues about its identity and what it stands for. In this comprehensive introduction, we'll explore the intricate relationship between appearance and brand representation, drawing insights from various domains, including marketing, psychology, and design.

Chapter 2: The Significance of Dress Codes at Work

1. Appearance as the First Touchpoint

Before a customer interacts with a brand—be it through using its products, engaging with its services, or navigating its digital platforms—they experience its appearance. Just as Solomon (1983) emphasized that clothing is a significant part of the social skin, brands use appearance as their social facade. This visual layer, whether encountered in a storefront, a website, or a product's packaging, forms the first impression, setting the stage for all subsequent interactions.

2. The Semiotics of Appearance

Semiotics, the study of signs and symbols and their use or interpretation, has profound implications for brand appearance. As highlighted by Eco (1976), every design choice, color palette, font, or logo becomes a signifier, pointing to a deeper signified meaning. Brands meticulously craft these elements to convey specific attributes, whether it's luxury, sustainability, innovation, or authenticity.

3. Appearance and Emotional Resonance

The visual elements of a brand do more than just convey information; they evoke emotions. As per the findings of Labrecque and Milne (2012), specific colors can elicit feelings ranging from trust to excitement. A luxury brand might use muted, elegant shades to evoke exclusivity, while a brand targeting youth might opt for vibrant hues reflecting energy and vivacity.

4. Consistency in Appearance for Brand Recognition

Consistency is a cornerstone of effective branding. As per the studies of Keller (1993), consistent visual representation across touchpoints reinforces brand recall and strengthens brand associations.

Whether it's a consistent logo placement, uniform color schemes, or a distinct brand voice, consistency in appearance makes a brand instantly recognizable amidst a sea of competitors.

5. Appearance Reflecting Evolution and Adaptability

While consistency is paramount, adaptability in appearance reflecting changing times, trends, and consumer preferences showcases a brand's evolution. As highlighted by Muzellec and Lambkin (2006), brands that successfully rebrand or tweak their appearance while retaining core elements showcase adaptability without alienating their loyal consumer base.

6. Appearance in the Digital Age

In today's digital age, a brand's appearance isn't limited to physical storefronts or tangible products. As per the insights of Gensler et al. (2017), digital platforms, websites, and social media profiles have become critical arenas where appearance plays a decisive role in user experience, engagement, and brand perception.

7. Cultural Sensitivity in Brand Appearance

With globalization, brands cater to diverse audiences spanning different cultures, backgrounds, and values. Ensuring that the brand's appearance resonates with diverse cohorts without causing unintentional offense is crucial. Studies by Zhang and Khare (2009) highlight the importance of cultural nuances in color perception and symbolism, emphasizing the need for cultural sensitivity in brand appearance.

Conclusion

Chapter 2: The Significance of Dress Codes at Work

In conclusion, the synergy between appearance and brand representation is undeniable. Brands, through their visual and sensory cues, tell stories, evoke emotions, and create lasting impressions. As they navigate the dynamic landscapes of global markets and digital transformations, understanding the profound impact of appearance becomes more crucial than ever. Brands that can seamlessly weave their core values and narratives into their appearance stand to gain lasting loyalty, recognition, and esteem in the eyes of their audience.

Offer guidance on creating a dress code that balances professionalism with comfort:

In the diverse and ever-evolving landscape of the modern workplace, striking the right balance between professionalism and comfort in dress codes has become an imperative. Historically, dress codes were often seen as rigid frameworks, delineating strict norms of appearance that employees were expected to adhere to. However, as the nature of work, workplace cultures, and societal norms have transformed, so too have perceptions of what constitutes appropriate work attire. The pendulum now swings towards a nuanced approach that champions individual expression while maintaining a cohesive organizational image. In this comprehensive introduction, we'll journey through the intricacies of drafting a dress code that harmoniously melds the aesthetics of professionalism with the comfort that today's workforce yearns for.

1. The Historical Perspective on Professional Attire

Historically, professional attire has often been closely linked with formality. As Rafaeli & Pratt (1993) noted, organizations used dress codes as instruments to foster a sense of unity, instill discipline, and project a specific corporate image. Suits, ties, and formal dresses were seen not merely as clothing but as symbolic representations of professionalism, authority, and commitment.

2. The Shift towards Casualization

The latter half of the 20th century witnessed the inception of a more relaxed approach to workplace attire. As per Sandikci & Ger (2007), the tech boom of the 1980s and 1990s, led predominantly by Silicon Valley, played a pivotal role in challenging the traditional paradigms of professional wear. The casual, often even quirky, attire of tech entrepreneurs and employees began to be associated with innovation, forward-thinking, and outside-the-box mentality.

3. The Psychology of Clothing

Clothing is more than just fabric; it has profound psychological implications. As established by Adam & Galinsky (2012), the clothes we wear can significantly impact our cognitive processes, self-perception, and mood. Their concept of "enclothed cognition" suggests that attire can either empower or constrain individuals, depending on its alignment with their comfort and identity.

4. The Multifaceted Nature of Comfort

Comfort in clothing is multidimensional. It's not just about the physical ease but also psychological comfort. For some, comfort might mean the tactile sensation of soft fabrics, while for others, it could signify the freedom to express their cultural, religious, or personal identity through attire (Roach-Higgins & Eicher, 1992).

5. The Need for Individuality and Inclusion

Modern workplaces are increasingly diverse, bringing together individuals from varied backgrounds, cultures, and lifestyles. A one-size-fits-all approach to dress codes risks marginalizing certain groups. As emphasized by Syed & Özbilgin (2009), an inclusive dress code acknowledges and respects these differences, promoting a sense of belonging and equity.

6. Crafting a Balanced Dress Code: Key Considerations

When drafting a dress code that balances professionalism with comfort, organizations need to consider:

- **Nature of the Business**: A tech startup's dress code might differ significantly from that of a law firm (Peluchette & Karl, 2007).

- **Client Interaction**: Roles that require frequent face-to-face interactions with clients might necessitate a more polished appearance (Rafaeli, 1993).

- **Safety and Practicality**: For some roles, specific attire or protective clothing might be essential for safety reasons (Tortora & Eubank, 2010).

- **Cultural Sensitivity**: Recognizing and respecting diverse cultural and religious attire is paramount (Syed & Kramar, 2010).

Conclusion

Crafting a dress code that melds professionalism with comfort is a delicate dance, requiring a deep understanding of both organizational objectives and individual needs. It's about recognizing that while attire plays a role in brand representation, the comfort and well-being of employees are equally, if not more, crucial. Organizations that can navigate this balance stand to foster a more inclusive, positive, and productive work environment.

The psychological impact of dressing appropriately:

The clothes we wear are more than just protective coverings for our bodies. They're a reflection of our identity, mood, culture, and even our psychological state. The very act of choosing what to wear on a given day or for a particular occasion can be a complex decision interwoven with a multitude of psychological implications. Furthermore, dressing appropriately, or in congruence with societal or situational expectations, can wield significant influence over our self-perception, confidence, and how others perceive and interact with us. In this comprehensive introduction, we will delve into the multifaceted psychological landscape that underscores the act of dressing appropriately.

A. Clothing as an Extension of Self

Dressing isn't merely a functional activity; it's a form of self-expression. According to Belk (1988), our possessions, including our clothing, can be viewed as a part of our extended self. When we choose items that resonate with our identity, values, or aspirations, we feel more authentic and self-congruent.

B. The Power of 'Enclothed Cognition'

Adam and Galinsky (2012) introduced the term "enclothed cognition" to describe the systematic influence clothes have on the wearer's psychological processes. Their research found that people embody the symbolic meaning of their clothes and their associated stereotypes. For instance, wearing a lab coat identified as a doctor's increased participants' attention compared to when it was described as a painter's coat.

C. Dressing for Success: Confidence and Competence

The adage "dress for success" encapsulates the link between attire and confidence. Kraus and Mendes (2014) found that wearing formal clothing made people feel more powerful, altering their cognitive processing. In professional settings, dressing appropriately can enhance perceived competence and credibility (Peluchette & Karl, 2007).

D. Social Acceptance and Conformity

Humans have an inherent desire to belong. Being attuned to societal or group norms, including dress codes, can facilitate social acceptance. As Asch (1956) illustrated in his seminal work on conformity, individuals often align with group standards, even if they personally disagree, to avoid social isolation.

E. Navigating Identity and Stereotypes

Dressing appropriately often involves navigating societal stereotypes. For instance, a study by Pratt and Rafaeli (1997) observed that female employees adopted masculine attire in male-dominated professions to gain acceptance. However, this alignment often comes at the cost of suppressing personal identity, leading to potential internal conflicts.

F. The Mood-Modulating Aspect of Dress

Clothes can influence mood and emotional state. Researchers like Bower (1981) have emphasized how congruence between attire and current emotional states (like wearing bright colors when happy) can amplify those emotions, while discord can have a moderating effect.

G. Cultural and Contextual Nuances

What's deemed appropriate varies across cultures and contexts. What's considered formal and suitable in a Western corporate setting might differ drastically from norms in an Eastern context (Kwon, 1994). Recognizing these nuances is essential to avoid cultural faux pas and to engage with diverse groups respectfully.

H. The Double-Edged Sword of Dressing Appropriately

While dressing in line with norms can confer numerous advantages, it's also essential to recognize its potential pitfalls. Overemphasis on appearance can lead to superficial judgments, overshadowing merit and substance (Dion, Berscheid, & Walster, 1972).

The act of dressing, especially doing so appropriately, is intricately tied to our psyche. It's a dance between expressing individuality and aligning with societal norms. As we navigate different situations, cultures, and stages of life, understanding the profound psychological impact of our sartorial choices can offer both empowerment and introspection.

How dress codes relate to company branding:

In the vast tapestry of corporate branding, elements like logos, taglines, and advertising campaigns are often the most prominently spotlighted. Yet, lurking subtly in this expansive branding vista, dress codes have emerged as potent, albeit understated, brand ambassadors. As companies grapple with the challenge of differentiating themselves in increasingly saturated markets, the way their employees dress has assumed a significant role, echoing the company's ethos, values, and identity. This comprehensive introduction unravels the intricate connections between dress codes and company branding, shedding light on how what employees wear can powerfully reflect and shape organizational narratives.

A. The Silent Communicator

Clothing speaks. While this might sound metaphorical, in the corporate realm, it's a reality. Every sartorial choice becomes a non-verbal cue, subtly transmitting messages about the company's culture, values, and ethos. As Solomon and Schopler (1982) posited, clothing is a form of social communication, carrying symbolic meanings that convey the wearer's (and by extension, the company's) identity.

B. Dress Codes as Brand Consistency Tools

One of the hallmarks of successful branding is consistency. Just as companies ensure logo uniformity across platforms, consistent employee attire projects a unified brand image. This consistency, as highlighted by Keller (1993), aids in reinforcing brand recall and strengthens the emotional connection with stakeholders.

C. Reflecting Corporate Culture and Values

The choice between formal suits, business casuals, or casual tees isn't arbitrary. It's often a mirror to the company's culture. Tech startups championing agility and innovation might favor casuals, emphasizing a break from traditional corporate molds. In contrast, banks might opt for formals, underscoring trustworthiness and professionalism (Rafaeli & Pratt, 1993).

D. Employee Attire as a Tangible Touchpoint

For many stakeholders, especially clients or customers, employees are the most tangible touchpoints of a company. Their attire becomes the physical embodiment of the brand, influencing perceptions and interactions. As per the findings of Forsythe (1990), clothing can significantly influence perceptions of credibility, trustworthiness, and approachability.

E. Dress Codes as Inclusivity Beacons

In today's globalized business landscape, companies are becoming increasingly diverse. An inclusive dress code that respects varied cultural, religious, and personal attire choices can project a brand image of respect, diversity, and global-mindedness (Syed & Kramar, 2010).

F. The Balance between Individuality and Branding

While dress codes serve branding purposes, companies also recognize the importance of individual expression. A flexible dress code allows employees to infuse personal elements, reflecting a brand that values individuality and creativity (Elfenbein & O'Reilly, 2007).

G. Dress Codes in the Digital Age

The digital transformation has reshaped brand representation. With virtual meetings becoming commonplace, 'camera-ready' attire (often formal on the top and casual at the bottom) is becoming popular. This shift underscores a brand that's both professional and adaptable to modern dynamics (Wiederhold, 2020).

H. Economic and Environmental Brand Implications

Chapter 2: The Significance of Dress Codes at Work

The type of clothing companies require or provide can also reflect economic and environmental brand values. Encouraging sustainable, ethically-made attire can align with a brand's eco-friendly stance (Joy et al., 2012).

In conclusion, dress codes, far from being mere guidelines on appropriate clothing, are intricately woven into the fabric of company branding. They communicate, resonate, and forge connections, echoing the company's stories and values. As the corporate landscape continues to evolve, understanding and leveraging the synergy between dress codes and branding will be pivotal for companies seeking to carve a distinctive identity.

Tips for creating a dress code policy:

Establishing a dress code policy for any organization isn't just about delineating what's acceptable attire and what's not. It's about understanding the organization's culture, respecting individuality, promoting inclusivity, and maintaining a professional image. An effective dress code policy serves multiple purposes: it communicates the company's values, boosts employee morale, and ensures that every staff member represents the organization appropriately. This comprehensive introduction will provide actionable tips for creating a dress code policy that balances organizational objectives with employee comfort and autonomy, all underpinned by evidence-based insights.

I. Understanding Organizational Needs and Culture

Before drafting a policy, it's essential to grasp the organization's ethos. Is it a laid-back startup or a formal financial institution? The dress code should reflect the nature and culture of the organization. Research by Pratt & Rafaeli (1997) underscores the importance of aligning dress codes with organizational culture to ensure cohesion and clarity.

II. Define the Objective Clearly

An effective policy starts with a clear objective. What does the organization hope to achieve with this dress code? Whether it's maintaining professionalism, ensuring safety, or fostering a team spirit, being clear about the goals can guide the policy's specifics (Peluchette & Karl, 2007).

III. Be Specific but Not Overly Prescriptive

While it's essential to provide clear guidelines, offering some flexibility can be beneficial. Instead of listing specific attire items, define the broader categories or the expected level of formality (Adams & Galinsky, 2012).

IV. Ensure Cultural and Religious Sensitivity

A globalized workplace often comprises diverse backgrounds. It's crucial to ensure the dress code doesn't inadvertently marginalize or discriminate against any group. This not only fosters inclusivity but also aligns with legal mandates in many jurisdictions (Syed & Kramar, 2010).

V. Account for Different Scenarios

Consider different events or days when the regular dress code might not apply, such as casual Fridays or specific occasions like company events. Having guidelines for these ensures clarity and consistency (Kwon, 1994).

VI. Highlight the Importance of Neatness and Hygiene

While focusing on the type of attire, don't neglect the importance of cleanliness and personal hygiene. These elements often have a more significant impact on professionalism than attire alone (Rafaeli & Pratt, 1993).

VII. Consider Practicality and Comfort

An effective dress code isn't just about appearance; it respects the comfort and practicality of the attire. If employees are uncomfortable, it can impede productivity and job satisfaction (Hannover & Kühnen, 2002).

VIII. Address Safety Concerns

In certain professions, attire isn't just about branding or professionalism; it's a safety concern. Ensure the dress code policy addresses any safety requirements specific to the job role or industry (Tortora & Eubank, 2010).

IX. Involve Employees in the Decision Process

Involving employees in the formulation of the dress code can ensure its acceptance and adherence. A participatory approach fosters a sense of ownership and can provide insights into employee needs and preferences (Dale, 2014).

X. Regularly Review and Update the Policy

The workplace, societal norms, and fashion evolve. Regularly revisiting and revising the dress code policy ensures it remains relevant and effective (Roach-Higgins & Eicher, 1992).

Chapter 2: The Significance of Dress Codes at Work

Crafting a dress code policy requires a thoughtful balance between defining organizational standards and respecting individual choices. It's not just about prescribing what employees should wear; it's about creating a cohesive, inclusive, and productive work environment. With the right approach, a dress code can be more than just a policy; it can be a testament to an organization's values, adaptability, and commitment to its employees.

Chapter 3: The Art of Dealing with Coworkers

Amidst the bustling corridors, coffee breaks, and cubicles of the corporate world lies the intricate maze of interpersonal relationships. These aren't just casual conversations around the water cooler or brief nods in the hallway. These are the relationships with coworkers - the very individuals you spend a significant portion of your life with. Navigating relationships with coworkers is an art, one that demands empathy, communication, understanding, and sometimes, a touch of diplomacy. In this comprehensive introduction to the art of dealing with coworkers, we will traverse the multifaceted pathways of workplace relationships, delving into their importance, challenges, and the strategies to foster positive and productive interactions.

1. The Centrality of Coworker Relationships

The significance of coworker relationships in the modern workplace can't be overstated. According to Morrison (2004), positive relationships with coworkers can significantly influence job satisfaction, commitment, and overall well-being. It's not just about camaraderie; it's about creating a supportive ecosystem that nurtures growth and collaboration.

Understanding the intricacies of the professional environment requires us to delve into one of its most foundational elements: coworker relationships. These relationships serve as the backbone of the workplace, dictating its dynamics, atmosphere, and productivity. When viewed from a holistic perspective, positive interactions with colleagues transcend mere cordiality, becoming critical drivers of job satisfaction, personal growth, and organizational success.

a) The Impact on Job Satisfaction and Performance

The correlation between coworker relationships and job satisfaction is strongly supported by empirical evidence. According to Sias (2009), employees who maintain positive relationships with their colleagues are more likely to experience job satisfaction, increased commitment to the organization, and enhanced personal well-being. Such positive relationships foster an environment of mutual trust and support, facilitating knowledge exchange, collaboration, and reduced work-related stress.

b) A Pillar of Organizational Culture

Coworker relationships significantly influence and are influenced by organizational culture. As Schein (2010) posited, shared experiences and interactions among employees give rise to a set of shared beliefs, values, and norms that constitute the organizational culture. Positive coworker relationships often indicate a healthy organizational culture characterized by mutual respect, open communication, and shared values.

c) Coworker Relationships and Knowledge Sharing

In today's knowledge-driven economy, the sharing of information and expertise is paramount. When employees share positive relationships, they are more inclined to exchange knowledge and assist one another. Cummings (2004) found that trust, borne out of positive coworker relationships, significantly influences knowledge sharing, ultimately enhancing team performance and innovation.

d) **Buffer Against Work-Related Stress**

The modern workplace, with its myriad challenges and pressures, can be a source of significant stress. Positive coworker relationships serve as a buffer against this stress. Research by Morrison (2004) suggests that supportive interactions with colleagues can mitigate feelings of isolation, providing emotional and instrumental support during challenging times.

e) **Influence on Career Growth and Development**

While skills and qualifications are essential, networking and relationships within the workplace often play a pivotal role in career advancement. Building and maintaining strong coworker relationships can lead to mentorship opportunities, endorsements, and collaborations, all of which can accelerate career growth (Seibert, Kraimer, & Liden, 2001).

Coworker relationships, with their intricate dynamics and profound implications, lie at the very heart of the professional ecosystem. Their centrality to multiple facets of the workplace— from personal well-being to organizational innovation— underscores the need for fostering positive, meaningful interactions. As the landscape of work continues to evolve, anchored by globalization and technological advancements, the timeless essence of human relationships remains ever pertinent, guiding the rhythms and flows of the workplace.

2. The Double-Edged Sword of Proximity

While proximity fosters familiarity and collaboration, it can also lead to conflicts. As Festinger et al. (1950) posited, physical closeness can lead to increased social interaction, which, while often positive, can also escalate into disputes if not managed appropriately.

In the intricate web of workplace dynamics, physical proximity to coworkers plays a paradoxical role. On the one hand, it has the potential to foster collaboration, spur creativity, and deepen relationships. On the other, it can give rise to conflicts, competition, and misunderstandings. Like a double-edged sword, proximity can be both a boon and a bane, depending on various factors. Let's delve deeper into the implications of this proximity and the research underpinning its effects.

a) **Fostering Collaboration and Teamwork**

Proximity can facilitate spontaneous interactions, allowing coworkers to discuss ideas, seek feedback, and collaborate more effectively. Kraut, Egido, and Galegher (1988) highlighted the role of physical closeness in promoting frequent communication, essential for collaboration, especially in team-based environments. The simple act of being in the same space can lead to "water cooler" moments, sparking innovation and creativity.

b) **Strengthening Interpersonal Relationships**

Regular face-to-face interactions, facilitated by proximity, can lead to stronger interpersonal bonds. According to Festinger, Schachter, and Back's (1950) social comparison theory, individuals often form bonds and friendships with those they encounter frequently. Over time, these interactions can result in deeper trust, understanding, and mutual respect.

c) **Heightened Potential for Conflict**

While proximity can enhance communication, it can also escalate misunderstandings and conflicts. Close quarters can amplify personality clashes, differences in working styles, and competition, potentially leading to disputes. As found by Wageman (1995), teams that share close physical spaces, while benefiting from improved communication, also face increased instances of conflict.

d) **Reduced Privacy and Autonomy**

Being in close proximity to coworkers can sometimes curtail an individual's sense of privacy and autonomy. Constant oversight, whether real or perceived, can lead to feelings of surveillance, reducing job satisfaction and potentially impacting performance. Altman (1975) postulated that individuals have a basic need for personal space and privacy, even in professional settings, and disruptions to this can lead to stress and discomfort.

e) **Influence on Organizational Dynamics**

Physical layout and proximity also influence broader organizational dynamics. For instance, being physically closer to decision-makers or senior management might provide certain teams or individuals with more influence, access to resources, or information. This spatial advantage, as highlighted by Zahn (1991), can significantly shape power dynamics within an organization.

Proximity in the workplace is a multifaceted construct, bringing both opportunities and challenges. While it serves as a catalyst for collaboration and relationship-building, it also necessitates effective conflict management strategies and an understanding of personal boundaries. Organizations, in their quest for optimizing workspace layouts and dynamics, must be cognizant of these dual implications, crafting strategies that harness the benefits of proximity while mitigating its potential drawbacks.

3. Understanding Different Personalities

Every individual is a unique blend of experiences, values, and personality traits. Recognizing and respecting these differences is the cornerstone of healthy coworker relationships. The Myers-Briggs Type Indicator (MBTI), as outlined by Myers & McCaulley (1985), offers insights into different personality types, aiding in understanding and collaboration.

The modern workplace is a mosaic of diverse personalities. It's a dynamic blend of varying perspectives, working styles, and temperaments. Recognizing and understanding these different personalities is not just an exercise in human psychology; it's a prerequisite for fostering collaboration, resolving conflicts, and promoting a harmonious working environment. Let's delve deeper into the significance of understanding personality diversity and the research underscoring its implications in the workplace.

a) Theoretical Frameworks on Personality

Numerous theoretical frameworks aim to categorize and understand human personalities. The Myers-Briggs Type Indicator (MBTI), based on Jungian psychology, categorizes individuals into 16 personality types based on four dichotomies: extraversion/introversion, sensing/intuition, thinking/feeling, and judging/perceiving (Myers & McCaulley, 1985). Another widely recognized framework is the Big Five personality traits, which includes openness, conscientiousness, extraversion, agreeableness, and neuroticism (Goldberg, 1990). Understanding these models can provide insights into how coworkers might think, behave, and interact.

b) **Implications for Team Dynamics**

The composition of team personalities can significantly influence team dynamics, productivity, and innovation. For instance, a team balanced with extroverts and introverts can harness both group discussions and individual reflections for problem-solving. Belbin (1981) proposed a team role model that emphasizes the importance of having diverse personality types in a team, each contributing uniquely to the team's success.

c) **Conflict Resolution and Communication**

Recognizing personality differences is vital for effective conflict resolution. Certain personalities may prefer direct confrontation, while others opt for more subtle, diplomatic approaches. Tjosvold (1991) suggests that understanding these nuances can lead to constructive conflict management, turning disagreements into opportunities for growth.

d) **Leadership and Motivation**

Leadership styles might resonate differently with various personalities. While some employees might feel motivated by assertive, directive leadership, others might thrive under a more collaborative and democratic leadership style. Understanding these distinctions is crucial for effective leadership and motivation (House, 1971).

e) **Promoting Inclusivity and Respect**

Acknowledging and valuing diverse personalities promotes inclusivity. It signals that every employee, regardless of their temperament or working style, is valued and respected. Such inclusivity can boost morale, job satisfaction, and overall workplace harmony (Cox, 1994).

Understanding different personalities in the workplace is akin to navigating a complex, dynamic puzzle. Each piece, representing an individual's unique personality, contributes to the larger picture. By recognizing and valuing these diverse personalities, organizations can foster a culture of mutual respect, collaboration, and innovation. The benefits of such understanding are manifold, spanning improved team dynamics, effective leadership, and a harmonious, inclusive workplace.

4. The Role of Effective Communication

Clear and open communication is the lifeblood of positive coworker relationships. It's not just about speaking; it's about listening and understanding. Active listening, a concept championed by Rogers and Farson (1957), emphasizes truly understanding the speaker's perspective, fostering mutual respect and reducing conflicts.

Effective communication acts as the linchpin that holds together the complex fabric of workplace interactions. In the context of coworker relationships, communication goes beyond the mere exchange of words—it is the vehicle for understanding, collaboration, conflict resolution, and relationship building. Properly understood and implemented, effective communication can transcend barriers, foster mutual respect, and promote a harmonious and productive workplace environment. Let's explore this fundamental aspect of coworker dynamics in greater detail.

a) **Understanding the Layers of Communication**

Chapter 3: The Art of Dealing with Coworkers

Communication is multifaceted. Mehrabian's (1971) seminal research suggests that only 7% of any message is conveyed through words, 38% through certain vocal elements, and 55% through non-verbal elements. Thus, effective communication is not just about what is said, but also how it is expressed and the body language that accompanies it.

b) **Active Listening: The Heart of Communication**

Active listening, as conceptualized by Rogers and Farson (1957), is an empathetic way of listening wherein the listener fully concentrates, understands, and responds to the speaker. This form of listening promotes understanding and validation, leading to trust and a deeper connection between coworkers.

c) **Feedback Mechanisms**

Constructive feedback is a pivotal component of effective communication. It offers clarity, reinforces positive behavior, and provides an avenue for growth and improvement. According to London (2003), feedback, when delivered appropriately, can significantly enhance job satisfaction and performance.

d) **Navigating Cultural and Generational Differences**

In today's diverse workplaces, understanding cultural and generational communication nuances is crucial. Hall's (1976) theory of high-context and low-context cultures sheds light on how different cultures rely on implicit versus explicit communication. Similarly, understanding generational perspectives, from Baby Boomers to Gen Z, can lead to more effective and inclusive communication strategies (Twenge, 2010).

e)   **The Role of Digital Communication**

In an era dominated by emails, video conferences, and instant messaging, mastering digital communication is imperative. While these tools offer convenience, they also present challenges, such as the lack of non-verbal cues. Walther's (1996) Social Information Processing theory highlights how individuals adapt to and build relationships through computer-mediated communication.

f)   **Non-verbal Communication and its Implications**

Gestures, facial expressions, and posture play a pivotal role in communication. According to Birdwhistell (1970), every facial and bodily gesture is part of the complex language of non-verbal communication, often conveying more than words.

Effective communication in the context of coworker relationships is both an art and a science. By understanding its various facets, from active listening to navigating digital communication, professionals can build stronger, more fruitful relationships in the workplace. As organizations become increasingly diverse and digitally connected, the role of effective communication in bridging gaps and building bonds becomes even more paramount.

5. Navigating Conflicts and Disagreements

Conflicts are inevitable. However, they don't necessarily spell disaster. Handled effectively, conflicts can lead to growth, innovation, and stronger relationships. Fisher & Ury's (1981) seminal work on principled negotiation provides valuable strategies to transform conflicts into opportunities.

Chapter 3: The Art of Dealing with Coworkers

Conflicts and disagreements, often perceived as obstacles in the workplace, can be transformative if approached correctly. They offer a chance to address underlying issues, foster understanding, and catalyze personal and organizational growth. In the realm of coworker relationships, navigating these conflicts is a nuanced process, requiring empathy, understanding, and effective communication. Let's delve into the intricacies of workplace conflicts and the strategies to navigate them effectively.

a) **Understanding the Root Causes**

Workplace conflicts can arise from a multitude of sources—misunderstandings, differences in values or priorities, competition, and personality clashes. Robbins and Judge (2018) categorize these conflicts into relationship, task, and process conflicts. Understanding the root cause can significantly aid in devising effective resolution strategies.

b) **The Constructive Side of Conflict**

Contrary to popular belief, not all conflict is detrimental. When managed appropriately, it can lead to beneficial outcomes. According to Jehn (1995), constructive or task-related conflicts can spur creativity, lead to better decision-making, and foster innovation by allowing diverse viewpoints to emerge.

c) **The Role of Emotional Intelligence**

Goleman (1995) posits that emotional intelligence, the ability to recognize, understand, and manage our emotions and those of others, plays a pivotal role in conflict resolution. Individuals with high emotional intelligence can navigate disagreements with empathy, ensuring that the resolution process is more collaborative and less adversarial.

d) Communication as the Key

Open, transparent, and effective communication is paramount in resolving conflicts. Fisher and Ury's (1981) principled negotiation approach from their seminal work, "Getting to Yes," emphasizes focusing on interests rather than positions, generating options for mutual gain, and using objective criteria for decision-making.

e) The Need for Neutral Mediation

In instances where conflicts escalate or become entrenched, the intervention of a neutral mediator can be beneficial. Mediators, as highlighted by Bercovitch and Jackson (2009), can facilitate communication, offer new perspectives, and guide parties towards a mutually beneficial resolution.

f) Promoting a Culture of Feedback

Regular feedback mechanisms can preemptively address potential conflict sources. By fostering an environment where feedback is encouraged and valued, organizations can ensure that grievances are addressed before they escalate into larger conflicts (London, 2003).

g) Training and Workshops

Investing in conflict resolution training and workshops can equip employees with the tools and strategies to navigate disagreements effectively. These sessions can cover various aspects, from effective communication techniques to understanding different cultural and personality-driven conflict styles (Augsburger, 1992).

Conflicts and disagreements, inherent in any collaborative environment, need not be viewed with apprehension. Instead, by understanding their nature and adopting effective resolution strategies, they can be transformed into opportunities for growth, understanding, and collaboration. In the delicate dance of coworker relationships, the ability to navigate conflicts gracefully is both a challenge and a reward, paving the way for a harmonious and productive workplace.

6. Fostering a Culture of Appreciation

Recognizing and appreciating coworkers' efforts can work wonders for workplace relationships. As per Herzberg's Two-Factor Theory (1968), recognition is a significant motivator, enhancing job satisfaction and interpersonal dynamics.

In the scope of coworker dynamics, a culture of appreciation plays a pivotal role in strengthening bonds, enhancing morale, and boosting productivity. Recognizing and valuating the contributions and worth of employees not only instills a sense of belonging but also drives them to consistently perform at their best. Let's explore the significance of fostering this culture and the research highlighting its multifaceted benefits.

a) The Psychological Impact of Recognition

Being acknowledged for one's contributions leads to a host of positive psychological outcomes. According to Deci, Vallerand, Pelletier, and Ryan (1991), appreciation and recognition serve as intrinsic motivators, enhancing job satisfaction, commitment, and overall well-being.

b) The Role of Appreciation in Team Dynamics

In team settings, mutual appreciation fosters an atmosphere of trust and collaboration. As per Tuckman's (1965) stages of group development, teams that consistently recognize each other's contributions tend to progress more rapidly through the 'storming' stage, achieving a harmonious 'performing' stage.

c) **Tangible and Intangible Forms of Appreciation**

Appreciation can be demonstrated in various ways, from monetary bonuses and promotions to verbal praise and tokens of gratitude. Herzberg's Two-Factor Theory (1968) suggests that while tangible rewards are powerful motivators, intangible forms of appreciation, such as recognition and responsibility, provide lasting job satisfaction.

d) **Appreciation and Organizational Commitment**

A direct correlation exists between appreciation and organizational commitment. Research by Eisenbeiss, Knippenberg, and Boerner (2008) suggests that employees who feel valued and recognized are more likely to be loyal, go the extra mile, and display organizational citizenship behaviors.

e) **Promoting Diversity and Inclusion through Appreciation**

A culture of appreciation also promotes diversity and inclusion. By recognizing and valuing the unique contributions of each individual, irrespective of their background, organizations send a powerful message of inclusivity (Cox, 1994).

f) **Challenges of Implementing a Culture of Appreciation**

While fostering a culture of appreciation has numerous benefits, challenges exist. Over-recognition or insincere praise can diminish the impact of genuine appreciation. Thus, it's crucial to ensure that recognition is both authentic and merited (Brun & Dugas, 2008).

Chapter 3: The Art of Dealing with Coworkers

Fostering a culture of appreciation is not merely an organizational strategy; it's a philosophy that recognizes the inherent worth of every individual. In the complex dynamics of coworker relationships, this culture serves as the glue that binds individuals together, creating a cohesive, motivated, and highly productive workforce. Through genuine recognition and valuing of contributions, organizations can unlock the vast potential of their most valuable asset—their employees.

7. The Dynamics of Teamwork

Working in teams brings its own set of challenges and rewards. Tuckman's (1965) stages of group development - forming, storming, norming, performing, and adjourning - offer insights into the evolution of team dynamics and strategies to foster cohesion and productivity.

Teamwork lies at the core of many organizational operations. In an increasingly interconnected world, the ability for diverse individuals to effectively collaborate can make the difference between success and stagnation. Delving into the dynamics of teamwork provides insights into the challenges and opportunities inherent in collective endeavors, and it showcases the importance of interpersonal skills in achieving shared goals. Let's explore the various facets of teamwork, supported by research and insights from academic literature.

a) The Stages of Team Development

Tuckman's (1965) stages of group development—forming, storming, norming, performing, and adjourning—provides a foundational framework to understand team progression. Each stage, from initial formation to task completion, brings its own challenges and growth opportunities, necessitating adaptive strategies to facilitate smooth transitions.

b) **The Role of Trust in Teams**

Trust acts as the bedrock of effective teamwork. Mayer, Davis, and Schoorman (1995) postulate that trust within teams arises from perceptions of ability, benevolence, and integrity of team members. High levels of trust can lead to increased information sharing, enhanced collaboration, and reduced conflicts.

c) **Diversity in Team Composition**

Diverse teams, comprising members from various backgrounds, genders, and disciplines, bring a rich tapestry of perspectives to the table. While they can face challenges related to communication and understanding, Cox and Blake (1991) argue that such diversity can lead to increased creativity and better decision-making.

d) **Communication within Teams**

Effective communication is pivotal in team settings. Edmondson (1999) highlights the importance of psychological safety in teams, enabling members to voice their opinions, share concerns, and ask questions without fear of retribution, thereby fostering open communication.

e) **Leadership in Team Dynamics**

The role of a team leader is not just to guide but also to inspire, motivate, and ensure alignment with organizational goals. Bass's (1985) transformational leadership theory sheds light on the qualities of leaders who can elevate their team's morale, motivation, and performance.

f) **Role Clarity and Task Distribution**

Ensuring that each team member has a clear understanding of their role and responsibilities is crucial. Role ambiguity can lead to overlaps, inefficiencies, and conflicts. According to Rizzo, House, and Lirtzman (1970), clear role definitions can significantly enhance job satisfaction and reduce the potential for intra-team conflicts.

g) **Feedback and Continuous Improvement**

Regular feedback, both positive and constructive, plays a pivotal role in team dynamics. It aids in aligning efforts, recognizing achievements, and identifying areas of improvement. London (2003) emphasizes the importance of feedback in driving performance improvements and fostering a culture of continuous learning.

Teamwork is a multifaceted dynamic, influenced by various interpersonal and organizational factors. By understanding the intricacies of team development, communication, trust, and leadership, organizations can optimize their team dynamics, driving enhanced collaboration, innovation, and productivity. In the landscape of coworker relationships, the nuances of teamwork illuminate the paths to collective achievement, emphasizing the age-old adage—united we stand, divided we fall.

8. Establishing Boundaries

While forging close relationships with coworkers is beneficial, it's also essential to establish boundaries. These boundaries, as highlighted by Petronio (2002) in the Communication Privacy Management theory, ensure a balance between personal space and collaborative openness.

In the bustling corridors of modern workplaces, establishing boundaries has become increasingly important. While collaboration, open communication, and teamwork are vital, it's equally crucial for individuals to delineate their personal and professional spheres, ensuring respect, privacy, and psychological well-being. Let's dive deep into the nuances of setting boundaries, underscored by academic insights and research.

a) **The Psychological Importance of Boundaries**

Boundaries are essential for maintaining mental health and self-identity. According to Derlega and Chaikin (1977), individuals need personal space and control over their environment to avoid stress, anxiety, and burnout. This can be especially pertinent in open-plan offices or environments where personal space is limited.

b) **Professionalism and Boundaries**

Maintaining a professional demeanor requires the establishment of appropriate boundaries. Clark (2010) posits that setting clear professional boundaries can prevent potential misunderstandings, protect one's professional reputation, and foster trust among colleagues.

c) **Avoiding Workplace Burnout**

With the rise of remote work and digital communication tools, the lines between personal and professional life can often blur. Setting boundaries in terms of working hours and availability can prevent burnout and ensure work-life balance. Research by Sonnentag, Binnewies, and Mojza (2010) highlights the importance of detaching from work during off-hours for recuperation and well-being.

d) **Handling Overly Intrusive Colleagues**

Chapter 3: The Art of Dealing with Coworkers

While openness is valued, there can be instances of colleagues becoming overly intrusive or crossing professional boundaries. Addressing such behaviors directly yet tactfully is essential. Ashforth, Kreiner, and Fugate (2000) discuss the strategies individuals adopt to manage identity threats and maintain boundary control.

e) The Role of Organizational Culture

The organization's culture plays a crucial role in defining accepted boundaries. A culture that respects individuality and personal space will inherently support boundary establishment. Schein's (1985) work on organizational culture and leadership highlights how underlying assumptions in an organization can influence boundary-related behaviors and expectations.

f) Empowering Employees through Autonomy

Granting employees autonomy allows them to set their own boundaries in terms of how they work, collaborate, and interact. According to Ryan and Deci's (2000) Self-Determination Theory, autonomy is a fundamental psychological need, leading to increased motivation, performance, and well-being.

g) Training and Workshops

Organizations can provide training sessions on the importance of boundaries, how to establish them, and how to respect those set by others. Such initiatives can foster a respectful and understanding workplace environment where boundaries are both acknowledged and upheld (Stone, 2005).

Establishing boundaries, while it may seem straightforward, is a nuanced endeavor that requires both individual and organizational effort.

By understanding the importance of personal and professional demarcations, organizations can cultivate environments where respect and professionalism coexist seamlessly with personal well-being. In the complex dance of coworker relationships, boundaries set the stage for harmonious and effective interactions.

Discuss the significance of a healthy work environment:

In today's rapidly changing corporate landscape, the focus on productivity, innovation, and growth often takes center stage. Yet, at the foundation of these corporate aspirations lies an elemental factor that significantly influences these outcomes: a healthy work environment. Establishing a conducive work atmosphere is not merely an ethical or legal imperative; it is an organizational necessity with profound implications for both employees and businesses. This introduction will explore the significance of a healthy work environment, its multifaceted components, and the cascading benefits it offers, drawing from various academic insights and research findings.

1. Defining a Healthy Work Environment

A healthy work environment goes beyond the physical safety and ergonomic design of the workspace. It encompasses a broader spectrum that includes psychosocial aspects, interpersonal relationships, organizational culture, work-life balance, and employee well-being. According to the World Health Organization (WHO), a healthy workplace is one where workers and managers collaborate to use a continual improvement process to protect and promote the health, safety, and well-being of all workers (WHO, 2010).

2. The Direct Impact on Employee Health

It's evident that the physical conditions of a workplace directly influence workers' health. Poorly designed workspaces can lead to musculoskeletal problems, impaired vision, and other health issues. Additionally, a stressful work atmosphere can lead to burnout, anxiety, and even chronic conditions like hypertension or heart diseases (Belkic et al., 2004). Ensuring a health-friendly environment is thus paramount to safeguarding employee health.

3. Enhancing Productivity and Performance

A healthy work environment translates to increased productivity. Workers operating in conducive environments are less likely to face disruptions from health issues or stress, leading to enhanced focus and performance. In a study conducted by Goetzel et al. (2004), it was found that health-related productivity losses cost U.S. employers $225.8 billion annually.

4. Reducing Absenteeism and Turnover

High turnover and absenteeism can be financially and operationally taxing for organizations. By ensuring a healthy workplace, organizations can significantly reduce these occurrences. Healthy employees are less likely to take sick days or seek employment elsewhere (Hemp, 2004).

5. The Role in Mental Well-being

Mental health, often overlooked, plays a critical role in overall employee well-being. A supportive work environment, recognition, fair treatment, and opportunities for professional growth contribute significantly to mental well-being (Mental Health Commission of Canada, 2012).

6. Implications for Organizational Reputation

In the age of information, businesses are under constant scrutiny. A company recognized for its healthy work environment can enjoy enhanced reputational benefits, attracting top-tier talent and potential business partnerships (Turban & Greening, 1997).

7. The Economic Rationale

While establishing a healthy work environment requires investment, the returns in terms of reduced healthcare costs, enhanced productivity, and decreased absenteeism offer a compelling economic rationale. According to Loeppke et al. (2009), every dollar invested in creating a healthy work environment can lead to a return on investment (ROI) ranging from $2.30 to $10.10.

A healthy work environment stands as a cornerstone of organizational success, playing a pivotal role in shaping employee well-being, productivity, and the overarching organizational culture. As the corporate world evolves, understanding, creating, and nurturing such environments will become increasingly crucial, with implications that ripple outwards, influencing not just organizational success but the broader societal fabric.

Share techniques for building camaraderie and trust:

In the intricate tapestry of organizational dynamics, the threads of camaraderie and trust weave patterns that largely dictate the quality of the workplace atmosphere, employee satisfaction, and even organizational output. The benefits of building strong interpersonal relationships in the workplace, rooted in mutual respect and trust, are manifold, ranging from enhanced team performance to improved morale and employee retention. Delving deep into the realm of organizational behavior and human interactions, this introduction explores techniques to cultivate camaraderie and trust, drawing on empirical research and expert insights.

1. Understanding the Foundations of Camaraderie and Trust

Trust, in the workplace context, is a belief in the reliability, truth, ability, or strength of colleagues. Camaraderie, on the other hand, denotes mutual trust and friendship among individuals who spend a lot of time together, especially at work. According to Dirks and Ferrin (2001), trust plays a pivotal role in predicting cooperation, job satisfaction, and commitment to the organization.

2. Open Communication

Clear, open, and frequent communication lays the groundwork for trust. Transparency in decision-making and operations reassures employees, makes them feel valued, and keeps misunderstandings at bay (Daft & Lengel, 1986).

3. Team-building Activities

Activities outside the standard work environment, such as retreats or workshops, can foster camaraderie. These events encourage employees to interact in informal settings, breaking down barriers and facilitating deeper connections (Tuckman, 1965).

4. Recognizing and Rewarding Efforts

Acknowledging hard work and achievements demonstrates that the organization values its employees, fostering trust and a sense of belonging. According to Herzberg's Two-Factor Theory (1959), recognition acts as a powerful motivator and contributor to job satisfaction.

5. Providing Opportunities for Professional Growth

Offering training, workshops, or courses signals that the organization is invested in the employee's future. This not only builds trust but also fosters loyalty and reduces turnover (Benson & Brown, 2007).

6. Encouraging Feedback

A culture that encourages feedback, both upwards and downwards, demonstrates openness and a genuine interest in improvement. Receiving and acting on feedback can significantly boost trust (London, 2003).

7. Flexibility and Work-life Balance

Recognizing and respecting employees' needs outside of work promotes trust. Work-life balance initiatives, flexible hours, and the possibility of remote work can be powerful trust-building tools (Kossek & Thompson, 2016).

8. Consistency in Actions and Promises

Trust is easily eroded when there's a mismatch between words and actions. Ensuring consistency between what is said and done is paramount to maintaining and building trust (Lewicki & Bunker, 1996).

9. Cultivating Psychological Safety

Chapter 3: The Art of Dealing with Coworkers

Creating an environment where employees feel safe to voice their opinions, take risks, and be themselves is crucial for building trust and camaraderie. Edmondson (1999) found that teams with psychological safety are more likely to harness the power of diverse ideas, leading to innovation and growth.

10. Promoting Diversity and Inclusion

Ensuring that the workplace is inclusive and values diversity fosters camaraderie. Recognizing and celebrating differences can lead to richer interactions and mutual respect (Cox & Blake, 1991).

Building camaraderie and trust is a multifaceted endeavor that demands intentionality, commitment, and continuous effort. By investing in interpersonal relationships, organizations stand to reap substantial dividends, from heightened productivity to a robust organizational culture. As we navigate the complexities of the modern workplace, the timeless values of trust and camaraderie serve as guiding lights, illuminating the path to collaborative success and shared achievement.

Introduce conflict resolution strategies:

In the dynamic theater of the workplace, where diverse personalities, goals, and interests coalesce, conflicts are almost inevitable. The existence of conflicts, however, isn't inherently detrimental; it's the management (or mismanagement) of these disagreements that can make or break teams and organizational outcomes. Effective conflict resolution can foster understanding, catalyze personal and collective growth, and lead to innovative solutions. Delving into this intricate topic, this introduction provides a comprehensive look into conflict resolution strategies, drawing upon a rich tapestry of research, insights, and academic findings.

1. Understanding the Nature of Conflict

Before embarking on resolution strategies, it's pivotal to understand the nature and types of conflict. Robbins and Judge (2018) categorized workplace conflicts into relationship, task, and process conflicts, each requiring a nuanced approach to resolution.

2. Active Listening

At the heart of many conflicts lies miscommunication or misunderstanding. Active listening, a technique where listeners fully concentrate, comprehend, and respond to the speaker, is often the first step in understanding the root cause of a conflict (Rogers & Farson, 1957).

3. Win-Win Negotiation

Fisher and Ury (1981) introduced the concept of principled negotiation in their seminal work, "Getting to Yes." They advocate for a win-win approach, where parties seek mutually beneficial solutions, focusing on underlying interests rather than entrenched positions.

4. Mediation by a Neutral Third Party

In scenarios where conflicts escalate or are deeply entrenched, introducing a neutral mediator can be beneficial. Mediators facilitate communication, encourage understanding, and guide disputing parties towards a mutually agreeable resolution (Moore, 2014).

5. Emphasizing Superordinate Goals

Sherif (1954) in his Robbers Cave experiment, highlighted how conflicting groups could collaborate when presented with superordinate (shared) goals. In organizational settings, emphasizing larger team or company goals can help realign conflicting individuals or subgroups.

6. Addressing the Conflict Promptly

Allowing conflicts to fester can make resolution harder. Addressing issues promptly, while they are still fresh, can lead to quicker and more amicable resolutions (Tjosvold, 2008).

7. Promoting a Culture of Feedback

Open feedback mechanisms can preempt potential conflict sources. Constructive feedback, delivered appropriately, can address grievances before they escalate into larger conflicts (London, 2003).

8. Implementing Team Contracts

Creating team contracts or charters that outline acceptable behaviors, communication norms, and decision-making processes can help in preempting and addressing conflicts (Rousseau, 1990).

9. Developing Emotional Intelligence (EI)

Goleman (1995) underscores the importance of emotional intelligence in interpersonal interactions, including conflict resolution. Individuals with high EI can navigate disagreements with empathy, ensuring a more collaborative approach to resolution.

10. Training and Workshops

Organizations can invest in conflict resolution training and workshops. Equip employees with tools, strategies, and a mindset conducive to resolving disagreements effectively (Rahim, 2002).

Conflicts, while challenging, present opportunities for growth, understanding, and innovation. Armed with effective resolution strategies, individuals and organizations can transform disagreements into catalysts for positive change. As the corporate world becomes increasingly interconnected and diverse, mastering the art of conflict resolution stands out as a critical skill, ensuring harmonious collaborations and paving the way for organizational success.

Present ideas for fostering a team-oriented culture:

Amidst the rapid pace of organizational evolution, businesses face an ever-pressing need to adapt, innovate, and outpace competitors. While technology, capital, and strategy undeniably play pivotal roles, there's a rising consensus that the heart of competitive advantage lies within an organization's culture, especially one that's team-oriented. A team-oriented culture celebrates collective achievements, prioritizes collaboration, and encourages every member to contribute towards shared objectives. This introduction aims to explore strategies for nurturing such a culture, fortified by scholarly insights and research findings.

1. The Essence of a Team-Oriented Culture

A team-oriented culture is rooted in the belief that "we are in this together." Such a culture doesn't just acknowledge the importance of teams but actively nurtures the conditions for them to flourish. As emphasized by Katzenbach and Smith (1993), high-performing teams can drive better results, promote innovative thinking, and heighten organizational adaptability.

2. Leadership as a Catalyst

Chapter 3: The Art of Dealing with Coworkers

Leaders play a crucial role in establishing and maintaining a team-oriented culture. Through their actions, priorities, and communication, leaders can inspire teamwork and set the tone for collaboration. Kouzes and Posner's (1987) transformative leadership model stresses the importance of leaders modeling the way, inspiring shared visions, and enabling others to act.

3. Celebrating Collective Achievements

One of the most tangible ways to reinforce a team-oriented culture is by celebrating collective wins. When team successes are highlighted and rewarded, it signals the organization's commitment to collaboration (Dyer, Dyer, & Dyer, 2013).

4. Cross-functional Collaboration

Encouraging departments and teams to work together on projects can break silos and foster a genuine appreciation for diverse perspectives. Such collaborations can lead to holistic solutions and foster a true spirit of teamwork (Edmondson & Nembhard, 2009).

5. Continuous Learning and Training

Investing in team-building exercises, workshops, and training can equip teams with the skills required to collaborate effectively. Tuckman's (1965) model of team development—forming, storming, norming, performing—offers insights into the stages teams undergo, emphasizing the importance of guidance and training at each phase.

6. Open Communication Channels

Transparency and open communication are pillars of a team-oriented culture. Teams should be encouraged to communicate openly, share feedback, and discuss challenges, ensuring alignment and collective problem-solving (West, 2012).

7. Empowering Teams

Empowerment is about granting teams the autonomy to make decisions, take ownership, and drive initiatives. An empowered team feels a greater sense of responsibility, commitment, and motivation to succeed (Kirkman & Rosen, 1999).

8. Encouraging Diversity and Inclusion

Diverse teams, with a mix of backgrounds, experiences, and perspectives, can drive innovation and robust problem-solving. A culture that values diversity inherently fosters teamwork by recognizing the strength in collective diversity (Cox & Blake, 1991).

9. Feedback Mechanisms

Instituting mechanisms for feedback, both within teams and from external stakeholders, can foster continuous improvement, alignment, and trust. Feedback, when constructive and solution-oriented, can bolster team cohesion (London, 2003).

10. Infusing Team Values in Hiring and Onboarding

Embedding team values right from the hiring and onboarding processes ensures that new members align with the team-oriented culture from the outset. This proactive approach can set the foundation for long-term collaboration (Pfeffer & Veiga, 1999).

Fostering a team-oriented culture is not a one-off initiative but a continuous journey that demands commitment, vision, and concerted efforts. As organizations navigate the challenges and opportunities of the modern business landscape, a culture that prioritizes teamwork can be a beacon, guiding them towards collaborative success, innovation, and unparalleled growth.

Conclusion

The art of dealing with coworkers isn't a static skill; it's an evolving journey, colored by changing dynamics, personalities, and organizational cultures. As workplaces continue to evolve, understanding the subtleties of these relationships becomes paramount. Through empathy, effective communication, and mutual respect, navigating the tapestry of workplace relationships can lead to a harmonious, productive, and fulfilling professional life.

Chapter 4: Mastering Customer Interactions

In an era dominated by technological advancements, digital platforms, and data-driven strategies, the essence of business success remains firmly rooted in a timeless principle: fostering positive customer interactions. As the frontline representatives of a brand, employees play a pivotal role in shaping these interactions, turning them into memorable experiences that can build loyalty, drive revenue, and foster long-term business relationships. This introduction provides a comprehensive exploration of mastering customer interactions, emphasizing its importance, strategies, and the multifaceted benefits it offers, supported by research findings and expert insights.

1. The Centrality of Customer Interactions

In the vast ecosystem of business operations, customer interactions stand out as pivotal moments that can make or break a brand's reputation. According to the Harvard Business Review, a positive customer experience can lead to a 140% increase in spending compared to a negative experience (Maxham III & Netemeyer, 2002). Thus, each interaction presents an invaluable opportunity to solidify the brand's value proposition.

Customer interactions stand as the touchpoints that define an organization's relationship with its client base. These moments, whether fleeting or sustained, can significantly influence perceptions, attitudes, and behaviors towards a brand. Delving deeper into the realm of these interactions reveals a landscape where each engagement is a potential pivot for loyalty, advocacy, or discontent. Supported by scholarly research and industry insights, this exploration underscores the central role customer interactions play in the broader tapestry of business operations and brand reputation.

a. The Anatomy of a Customer Interaction

A customer interaction is not just a mere transaction; it is an experience, a dialogue between the customer and the brand. From the initial greeting to the concluding remarks, each facet of the interaction contributes to the overall customer perception (Bitner, 1990). Whether it's a face-to-face engagement in a store, an online chat session, or a phone conversation, the quality of interaction can leave a lasting impression.

b. The Ripple Effect of Interactions

Positive customer interactions often extend beyond the immediate engagement. Customers who have positive experiences are more likely to share their encounters through word of mouth, online reviews, and social media, amplifying the impact of a singular positive interaction (East et al., 2007). Conversely, negative interactions can lead to detrimental ripple effects, with customers potentially dissuading others from engaging with the brand.

c. Emotional Resonance and Memory

Emotion plays a significant role in shaping memories. Interactions that evoke strong positive emotions can lead to memorable experiences, enhancing customer loyalty and affinity. On the contrary, interactions that elicit negative emotions can deter customers from future engagements (Laros & Steenkamp, 2005).

d. The Business Impact

The centrality of customer interactions extends to tangible business outcomes. Research has indicated that companies emphasizing superior customer experiences achieve revenue growth at a rate 4-8% above their market (Bain & Company, 2016). Such findings reiterate the profound influence of individual interactions on broader business metrics.

e. Shaping Brand Perceptions

Brands are not just logos or taglines; they are the amalgamation of experiences and perceptions. Customer interactions, being direct engagements with the brand, play a pivotal role in shaping these perceptions. Consistent, positive interactions can solidify a brand's positioning, while inconsistent engagements can erode brand equity (Keller, 1993).

The centrality of customer interactions in today's business landscape cannot be overstated. As the touchpoints that bridge brands with their audiences, these interactions bear the weight of crafting perceptions, influencing decisions, and driving business outcomes. In the evolving arena of customer-centricity, understanding, valuing, and mastering customer interactions stands out as a cardinal imperative for sustained brand success.

2. The Evolution of Customer Expectations

With the proliferation of technology, customers today are more informed, empowered, and have heightened expectations. A study by Salesforce revealed that 76% of customers expect companies to understand their needs and expectations (Salesforce, 2019).

Chapter 4: Mastering Customer Interactions

Customer expectations have undergone seismic shifts over the past few decades, driven largely by technological advancements, globalized markets, and the proliferation of information. The digital age has ushered in a new breed of consumers—empowered, informed, and with heightened anticipations from brands. This exploration offers a deep dive into the transformation of customer expectations, elucidating their origins, current state, and implications, fortified by scholarly findings and expert insights.

a. The Historical Context

Historically, the seller was the primary source of product information, and customers had limited means to verify claims or compare offerings. With the advent of the Internet and subsequent digital technologies, the information asymmetry began to tilt in favor of the consumer (Peterson et al., 1997).

b. Rise of the Digital Consumer

The digital revolution has made a plethora of information accessible at consumers' fingertips. Comparison shopping, online reviews, and social media insights allow customers to make informed decisions like never before (Chevalier & Mayzlin, 2006). As a result, they demand more transparency, authenticity, and value from brands.

c. The Demand for Personalization

With the ability to tailor digital experiences, consumers now expect personalization as a standard service, not a luxury. According to a study by Accenture (2018), 91% of consumers are more likely to shop with brands that recognize and provide relevant offers and recommendations.

d. The Expectation of Omni-channel Experiences

Today's consumers fluidly move between online and offline channels. They expect seamless integration across touchpoints, whether shopping online, in-store, or through mobile apps (Verhoef et al., 2015).

e. Instant Gratification and Speed

In the age of Amazon's same-day deliveries and real-time customer support, patience is waning. The expectation of immediate responses and fast services has become a norm, largely propelled by technological innovations that have made such speed feasible (PwC, 2018).

f. Ethical and Sustainable Expectations

Modern consumers are not just buying products or services; they are increasingly aligning with brands that mirror their values. Ethical business practices, sustainability, and corporate responsibility have become significant drivers of brand preference (Carrington et al., 2010).

g. Co-creation and Participation

Today's consumers desire a more active role in their engagements with brands. From product development to marketing campaigns, they seek avenues for co-creation, desiring experiences that are interactive and participatory (Prahalad & Ramaswamy, 2004).

The evolution of customer expectations underscores a broader narrative of empowerment and informed decision-making. For businesses, keeping pace with these shifting expectations is not merely advantageous—it's imperative for survival. As the contours of consumer anticipations continue to evolve, businesses that listen, adapt, and innovate in alignment with these expectations stand to build enduring relationships, foster loyalty, and drive sustained success.

3. The Art of Active Listening

Active listening, characterized by fully concentrating, understanding, responding, and remembering what the customer is saying, is a cornerstone of effective customer interactions. Such genuine attentiveness can differentiate a brand in a crowded marketplace (Rogers & Farson, 1957).

The bedrock of any meaningful interaction is communication, and within this dynamic, the role of active listening is paramount. In customer interactions, the ability to truly hear, comprehend, and respond to customers' needs, concerns, and feedback not only fosters trust but can also serve as a differentiator in a saturated market. This exploration delves into the nuances of active listening, elucidating its significance, its components, and its potential to transform customer interactions, fortified by scholarly insights and expert commentary.

a. What is Active Listening?

Active listening goes beyond mere hearing; it encompasses understanding and processing the information being shared and offering appropriate feedback. It is an intentional act, requiring full concentration and genuine engagement (Rogers & Farson, 1957).

b. The Components of Active Listening

- **Attending**: This involves being fully present in the interaction, showcasing interest through non-verbal cues like maintaining eye contact and nodding (Birdwhistell, 1970).

- **Reflecting**: Paraphrasing or summarizing what the customer has said, ensuring the message's accuracy and demonstrating understanding (Gordon, 1977).

- **Clarifying**: Asking open-ended questions to gather more information or gain clarity on specific points (Brownell, 1987).

- **Responding**: Offering appropriate feedback, solutions, or next steps based on the customer's communication (Bodie et al., 2008).

c. The Role of Empathy in Active Listening

Empathy stands as a cornerstone in active listening. It involves understanding the customer's emotions, offering validation, and demonstrating genuine concern. This empathetic approach can significantly enhance the quality of customer interactions (Eisenberg & Miller, 1987).

d. The Business Implications of Active Listening

Active listening has profound implications for businesses. It can lead to better problem resolution, enhanced customer satisfaction, and increased loyalty. A study by Weger et al. (2010) found that active listening can significantly influence perceptions of trust and understanding.

e. Barriers to Active Listening

There are several barriers that can hinder active listening in customer interactions, including distractions, preconceived notions, or emotional biases. Recognizing and mitigating these barriers is essential to ensure genuine engagement (Nichols, 1957).

f. Training and Skill Development

Active listening, while intuitive to some, is a skill that can be honed with training. Regular workshops, role-playing, and feedback sessions can enhance employees' active listening abilities, ensuring more effective customer interactions (Rautalinko & Lisper, 2004).

In the intricate dance of customer interactions, the art of active listening stands out as a crucial element. It has the power to turn mundane engagements into memorable experiences, foster trust, and build enduring relationships. As businesses seek to navigate the complexities of the modern market, active listening offers a path to genuine connection, understanding, and mutual growth.

4. Personalization: Beyond a Buzzword

Personalized experiences, tailored to individual customer preferences and histories, can significantly enhance customer satisfaction. McKinsey's research indicates that personalization can reduce acquisition costs by up to 50%, lift revenues by 5-15%, and increase marketing spend efficiency by 10-30% (Bughin & Chui, 2010).

In an increasingly interconnected world where businesses grapple for consumer attention, personalization has emerged as a key differentiator. Far from being a fleeting trend, personalization stands as a testament to a brand's commitment to understanding and valuing its customers. This in-depth exploration delves into the evolution, significance, and application of personalization in customer interactions, enriched by scholarly insights and practical examples.

a. Understanding Personalization

At its core, personalization is the art and science of tailoring experiences, products, or services to fit individual consumer preferences and behaviors. It's about recognizing the unique attributes of each customer and delivering a bespoke experience that resonates (Peppers & Rogers, 1997).

b. The Driving Forces Behind Personalization

- **Technological Advancements**: With the advent of AI, machine learning, and big data analytics, businesses can now harness vast amounts of customer data to derive insights and craft personalized experiences (Schwartz et al., 2017).

- **Evolving Consumer Expectations**: Modern consumers expect more than generic interactions. They crave recognition, relevance, and experiences that mirror their preferences (Accenture, 2018).

c. The Multifaceted Benefits of Personalization

- **Enhanced Customer Loyalty**: Personalized experiences can foster deeper connections, leading to increased brand loyalty and customer retention (KPMG, 2020).

- **Higher Conversion Rates**: Tailoring offerings to individual preferences can lead to higher engagement and increased sales (Gartner, 2018).

- **Streamlined Marketing Efforts**: Personalized marketing campaigns tend to yield better results as they cater to specific customer segments, leading to improved ROI (McCormick, 2016).

d. The Challenges of Personalization

While the rewards are evident, businesses also grapple with challenges in personalization:

- **Data Privacy Concerns**: As businesses gather more data, concerns about privacy and data misuse rise. It's essential to strike a balance between personalization and data privacy (Martin, 2018).

- **Over-personalization**: Overdoing personalization can make interactions feel invasive, defeating its purpose (Bleier & Eisenbeiss, 2015).

e. The Future of Personalization

The journey of personalization is just beginning. Emerging technologies and shifting consumer dynamics point towards an even more tailored future:

- **Hyper-Personalization**: Going beyond traditional data points, brands will use real-time data to offer hyper-personalized experiences (Meyer & Schwager, 2007).

- **Integration of Augmented Reality (AR) and Virtual Reality (VR)**: These technologies will offer personalized immersive experiences (Huang & Rust, 2018).

Personalization stands as a beacon of customer-centricity in the modern business landscape. By recognizing and valuing each customer's uniqueness, businesses can foster genuine connections, drive loyalty, and create memorable brand experiences.

5. Harnessing Technology to Enhance Interactions

From CRM systems to AI-driven chatbots, technology can play a pivotal role in enhancing customer interactions. These tools, when used judiciously, can provide timely information, streamline processes, and offer round-the-clock assistance, greatly enhancing the customer experience (Marr, 2016).

In the rapidly evolving world of digital engagement, technology has emerged as both a catalyst and a conduit, transforming the landscape of customer interactions. From enabling personalized experiences to facilitating real-time communication, technology plays an indispensable role in amplifying the quality and reach of brand-consumer engagements. This detailed exploration delves into the intertwining realms of technology and customer interactions, fortified by scholarly perspectives and industry insights.

a. Historical Landscape of Technological Interventions

The relationship between technology and customer interactions isn't new. From the invention of the telephone, which revolutionized real-time communication, to the advent of email, technology has consistently redefined the way businesses interact with customers (Aydin & Özer, 2005).

b. Artificial Intelligence (AI) and Machine Learning

- **Chatbots and Virtual Assistants**: AI-driven chatbots offer customers immediate, 24/7 support, answering queries and solving issues in real-time (Zhang et al., 2019).

- **Predictive Analysis**: Machine learning algorithms can analyze historical customer data to predict future behaviors, enabling brands to proactively cater to customer needs (Ngai et al., 2009).

c. Augmented Reality (AR) and Virtual Reality (VR)

AR and VR offer immersive brand experiences. Whether it's virtually trying on clothes or experiencing a product before purchase, these technologies blur the lines between the digital and physical worlds, enhancing customer interactions (Pantano et al., 2017).

d. Internet of Things (IoT)

IoT devices, from smart home assistants to wearable tech, open new avenues for businesses to interact with customers, providing real-time data, facilitating instant feedback, and crafting tailored experiences (Porter & Heppelmann, 2014).

e. Omni-channel Platforms

In the age of digital consumers, businesses are leveraging omni-channel strategies to ensure consistent and seamless interactions across various touchpoints, be it in-store, online, or via mobile apps (Verhoef et al., 2015).

f. Data Analytics and Personalization

Harnessing big data analytics allows brands to understand customer behaviors, preferences, and trends in depth. Such insights are pivotal for crafting hyper-personalized interactions, significantly enhancing customer satisfaction (Huang & Rust, 2018).

g. Challenges and Ethical Considerations

While technology offers immense potential, it also brings challenges:

- **Data Privacy and Security**: With increased data collection, businesses face the challenge of ensuring data privacy and security (Martin, 2018).

- **Over-reliance on Technology**: Relying too heavily on technology can sometimes alienate customers, especially if they seek genuine human interactions (Davenport et al., 2019).

The confluence of technology and customer interactions offers boundless opportunities for brands to innovate, delight, and forge deeper relationships. By judiciously harnessing technology while staying attuned to customer needs, businesses can craft interactions that resonate, inspire loyalty, and drive growth.

6. Training and Equipping Teams

Equipping customer-facing teams with the requisite skills, information, and tools is vital. Regular training sessions that cover product knowledge, communication skills, and problem-solving techniques can ensure consistent and positive customer interactions (Parasuraman et al., 1985).

In the landscape of customer interactions, frontline staff often stand as the embodiment of a brand's promise, values, and ethos. Their competence, attitude, and approach can significantly influence customer perceptions and, by extension, brand loyalty. Given this pivotal role, it becomes imperative for businesses to invest in training and equipping their teams adequately. This in-depth exploration discusses the nuances, significance, and strategies related to empowering customer-facing teams, underpinned by scholarly findings and industry insights.

Chapter 4: Mastering Customer Interactions

a. The Imperative of Training

Proper training ensures that customer interactions are consistent, efficient, and in line with brand standards. Well-trained employees are not only adept at handling operational aspects but can also manage emotional nuances, address concerns, and foster positive experiences (Hayes, 2008).

b. Components of Effective Training

- **Technical Skills**: Equipping teams with the knowledge and skills required to use tools, software, and systems ensures smooth operations (Nankervis & Compton, 2006).

- **Soft Skills**: Emphasizing communication, empathy, and problem-solving allows teams to manage diverse customer scenarios effectively (Riggio, 1986).

- **Brand Alignment**: Ensuring that every team member understands the brand's mission, values, and promises guarantees that customer interactions reflect the brand's essence (Mitchell, 2002).

c. The Role of Continuous Learning

The dynamics of customer interactions are continually evolving. Regular training sessions, workshops, and feedback loops ensure that teams stay updated with the latest products, services, trends, and tools (Aguinis & Kraiger, 2009).

d. Empowering Teams with the Right Tools

Beyond training, providing teams with cutting-edge tools and technologies can elevate the quality of customer interactions. For instance, Customer Relationship Management (CRM) systems can offer insights into customer history, preferences, and pain points, enabling tailored interactions (Trainor et al., 2014).

e. Creating a Feedback-Driven Culture

Encouraging a culture where teams regularly receive and act upon feedback—both from customers and peers—fosters continuous improvement. Such an environment not only enhances skills but also boosts team morale and motivation (London, 2003).

f. Simulation and Role-Playing

Simulating real-life customer scenarios through role-playing can be an effective training technique. It offers teams a safe environment to practice, make mistakes, and learn, ensuring they are better prepared for real-world situations (Girard & Pinar, 2019).

g. Addressing Challenges and Providing Support

It's essential to recognize that customer-facing roles can be stressful. Providing teams with resources, counseling, and support mechanisms ensures their well-being, leading to more genuine and positive customer interactions (Grandey et al., 2004).

Training and equipping customer-facing teams is not a one-time activity but an ongoing commitment. As businesses aspire to create memorable brand experiences, investing in their frontline ambassadors becomes a strategic imperative. A well-trained, empowered, and supported team can be the difference between a fleeting transaction and a lasting brand relationship.

7. Handling Difficult Situations with Grace

Not all customer interactions are smooth sailing. Handling complaints, feedback, or issues with empathy, promptness, and professionalism can often turn challenging situations into loyalty-building opportunities (Heskett et al., 1997).

In the area of customer interactions, not every engagement follows a seamless trajectory. Difficult situations, challenging customers, and unforeseen issues are all par for the course. How frontline staff navigate these waters can significantly influence brand perceptions and customer loyalty. Handling such situations with grace, empathy, and professionalism is pivotal. This detailed exploration delves into strategies and best practices for managing difficult situations, drawing from academic research and industry benchmarks.

a. The Nature of Difficult Situations

From irate customers to service failures, frontline teams encounter various challenges. These situations can be exacerbated by external pressures, such as cultural misunderstandings or high-stress environments (Hartel et al., 1999).

b. The Importance of Emotional Intelligence (EI)

EI, the ability to recognize, understand, and manage our own emotions as well as recognize, understand, and influence the emotions of others, is critical in navigating difficult situations. High EI enables staff to empathize with customers, maintain composure, and arrive at solutions more effectively (Salovey & Mayer, 1990).

c. Active Listening and Validation

Actively listening to customer concerns and validating their feelings can deescalate tensions. By showing customers that they are heard and understood, frontline staff can build bridges and pave the way for constructive solutions (Weger et al., 2010).

d. Solution-Oriented Approach

Transitioning from problem identification to solution generation is essential. Training teams to think proactively about remedies, offering alternatives, and being transparent about what can (and cannot) be done can foster customer trust (Bitner et al., 1990).

e. Apologizing Authentically

A genuine apology, devoid of defensiveness or blame-shifting, can have a powerful impact. Recognizing mistakes and expressing genuine remorse can go a long way in mending fences (Davidow, 2003).

f. Seeking Feedback for Continuous Improvement

Encouraging customers to share feedback about their experience, especially in difficult situations, can offer valuable insights. This feedback can be a cornerstone for training, refining approaches, and preventing future issues (Maxham, 2001).

g. Regular Training and Role-Playing Scenarios

Immersing frontline staff in simulated challenging situations can bolster their confidence and equip them with tools to handle real-world scenarios more effectively (Van Dijk & Van Dick, 2009).

h. Managerial Support and Debriefing

After handling a tough situation, frontline staff might benefit from debriefing sessions where they can discuss the incident, express their feelings, and receive managerial support. Such interventions can mitigate stress and burnout (Grandey et al., 2004).

Difficult situations in customer interactions are inevitable. However, with the right strategies, training, and support mechanisms, these challenges can be transformed into opportunities for growth, learning, and forging deeper customer relationships.

8. Measuring and Continuously Improving

Incorporating feedback mechanisms, such as surveys, reviews, and analytics, can offer invaluable insights into the quality of customer interactions. These insights can then drive continuous improvements, ensuring that businesses evolve in line with customer expectations (Reichheld, 2003).

Continuous improvement is a principle that extends seamlessly into the realm of customer interactions. Just as industries innovate their products, services, or processes, the approach to customer interactions must also evolve. By measuring key metrics and identifying areas of enhancement, businesses can deliver unparalleled service excellence. This comprehensive delve into the art and science of measurement and continuous improvement in customer interactions blends scholarly insights with actionable best practices.

a. The Imperative of Measurement

In the words of management guru Peter Drucker, "What gets measured gets improved." This mantra holds especially true in customer interactions where measurement can provide insights into strengths, gaps, and opportunities for enhancement (Drucker, 1954).

b. Key Metrics in Customer Interactions

- **Customer Satisfaction (CSAT)**: Typically gauged post-interaction, CSAT scores provide immediate feedback on the customer's experience (Oliver, 1997).

- **Net Promoter Score (NPS)**: An indicator of customer loyalty, NPS measures the likelihood of customers recommending a business to others (Reichheld, 2003).

- **Customer Effort Score (CES)**: This metric evaluates how easy it was for the customer to achieve their desired outcome, capturing the efficiency and seamlessness of the interaction (Morgan & Rego, 2006).

c. Leveraging Technology for Measurement

Modern tools like CRM systems, feedback platforms, and analytics software offer robust capabilities for capturing, analyzing, and interpreting customer interaction data in real-time, facilitating agile responses (Greenberg, 2010).

d. The Role of Feedback Loops

- **Customer Feedback**: Encouraging customers to share their experiences, both positive and negative, provides actionable insights for improvement (Aaker et al., 2004).

- **Employee Feedback**: Frontline staff, being the direct interface with customers, often possess valuable perspectives on what works and what could be enhanced (London, 2003).

e. Training and Upskilling

Based on measurement insights, continuous training sessions can be tailored to address specific gaps, introduce new tools or techniques, and reinforce best practices (Goldstein & Ford, 2002).

f. Process Refinement and Innovation

An iterative approach to customer interactions involves revisiting and refining processes, experimenting with novel techniques, and staying attuned to evolving customer expectations and industry trends (Deming, 1986).

g. Celebrating Successes and Learning from Shortcomings

While it's vital to address and rectify areas of improvement, celebrating successes boosts morale, fosters motivation, and sets a benchmark for excellence (Cameron & Lavine, 2006).

Continuous improvement in customer interactions isn't just about rectifying shortcomings—it's about striving for excellence, anticipating and shaping customer expectations, and forging meaningful, lasting relationships. In a world inundated with choices, the quality of customer interactions can be the differentiating factor that sets a brand apart.

Emphasize the role of customers in a business's success:

Customers, often heralded as the backbone of any enterprise, undeniably steer the trajectory of a business's success. From influencing product evolution to dictating market reputation, their role is multifaceted and monumental. Recognizing and valuing this centrality of customers is not just good etiquette—it's sound business strategy. This comprehensive analysis illuminates the pivotal role of customers in a business's success, merging scholarly insights with practical business wisdom.

I. Economic Impact of Loyal Customers

Loyal customers are the lifeblood of any sustainable business model. They not only provide consistent revenue but are also more likely to try new products and forgive minor transgressions (Reichheld & Sasser, 1990).

II. The Power of Word-of-Mouth

Customers serve as unofficial brand ambassadors. Positive word-of-mouth can significantly amplify a business's reach and reputation, while negative feedback can have detrimental effects on its image (East et al., 2007).

III. Customers as Co-Creators

Modern businesses are recognizing customers as partners in co-creating value. Through feedback, customization options, and interactive platforms, customers now actively shape products, services, and brand narratives (Prahalad & Ramaswamy, 2004).

IV. The Feedback Loop and Continuous Improvement

Constructive feedback from customers serves as a compass for businesses, directing product enhancements, service adjustments, and overall improvements (Anderson & Mittal, 2000).

V. Customers and Organizational Learning

Through their interactions, feedback, and behavior, customers indirectly educate businesses about market trends, emerging needs, and evolving preferences, fostering organizational agility and adaptability (Argyris, 1977).

VI. The Role of Customers in Branding and Identity

The perception and reputation of a brand are, in large part, reflections of its customers' opinions and experiences. Hence, customers play a crucial role in shaping, reinforcing, or challenging a brand's identity (Holt, 2002).

VII. Navigating Market Uncertainties

In uncertain markets, a loyal customer base can provide businesses with stability, predictability, and resilience, acting as a buffer against external shocks and challenges (Lemon et al., 2002).

In the grand tapestry of business success, customers are not just mere threads but the very fabric that gives it form, color, and character. Recognizing, valuing, and nurturing this pivotal relationship is paramount for businesses aspiring for longevity, growth, and resonance in their respective markets.

Share communication strategies to enhance customer interactions:

Communication stands as the cornerstone of all meaningful interactions, and in the context of customer interactions, its importance is magnified. Effective communication can shape perceptions, foster trust, and pave the way for enduring relationships. Conversely, miscommunication can lead to dissatisfaction, misperceptions, and lost opportunities. Herein, we delve into nuanced strategies aimed at elevating customer interactions, backed by scholarly research and industry insights.

I. Active Listening: The Silent Powerhouse

Active listening involves not just hearing what the customer is saying, but genuinely understanding and processing their message. It's the difference between a shallow nod and a deep acknowledgment (Weger et al., 2010).

II. Clarity and Conciseness

Confusion often roots in verbose or ambiguous communication. Ensuring clarity and brevity in interactions reduces misunderstandings and enhances comprehension (Cardon, 2010).

III. Empathy: The Emotional Connect

Conveying genuine empathy in customer interactions can bridge emotional gaps and foster connections. Customers feel valued when they sense that their emotions are recognized and respected (Dixon et al., 2010).

IV. Personalization: Beyond a Name

While addressing customers by their names is a good start, true personalization involves tailoring interactions based on individual customer profiles, history, and preferences (Bleier & Eisenbeiss, 2015).

V. Effective Use of Non-Verbal Cues

Body language, facial expressions, and tone of voice complement verbal communication, reinforcing the message and setting the interaction's emotional tone (Burgoon et al., 1989).

VI. Utilizing Feedback Loops

Chapter 4: Mastering Customer Interactions

Encouraging feedback and acting on it sends a clear message to customers: their voice matters. Regularly integrating feedback into communication strategies ensures continual refinement (Mohr & Nevin, 1990).

VII. Addressing Customer Concerns Proactively

Anticipating and addressing concerns before they escalate demonstrates foresight and a commitment to customer welfare. Proactive communication can mitigate potential dissatisfaction (Gilly & Gelb, 1982).

VIII. Incorporating Storytelling

Narratives and stories make communication relatable and memorable. When relevant to the interaction, sharing anecdotes or brand stories can create a deeper connection with customers (Lundqvist et al., 2013).

IX. Use of Positive Language

Replacing negative phrases with positive alternatives can shift the trajectory of a conversation. For instance, instead of saying "We can't do this," saying "What we can do is..." offers a solution-oriented approach (Higgins, 1987).

Mastering the art of communication in customer interactions is an ongoing journey. However, with deliberate strategies and a genuine commitment to understanding and serving customers, businesses can craft interactions that resonate, delight, and endure.

Introduce techniques for handling challenges and difficult situations:

Customer-facing roles often present a myriad of challenges that can range from minor misunderstandings to intense confrontations. How these challenges are managed can deeply influence a customer's perception of a brand. Effective techniques, underpinned by psychological and communicative principles, can transform these challenging interactions into opportunities for deepened trust and loyalty. This segment offers an in-depth look into strategies fortified by academic research and field-tested practices.

I. Stay Calm and Composed

In the face of challenging situations, maintaining one's composure is pivotal. By staying calm, you can think more clearly, respond more effectively, and prevent the situation from escalating (Gross, 2002).

II. Practice Reflective Listening

Reflective listening involves mirroring back the customer's statements to demonstrate understanding. This technique can clarify misconceptions and assure the customer that they are being heard (Rogers & Farson, 1957).

III. Apologize Genuinely

A sincere apology can go a long way in mending frayed emotions. Acknowledging a mistake and expressing regret can rebuild trust and pave the way for solutions (Fehr & Gelfand, 2010).

IV. Avoid Blame Games

Chapter 4: Mastering Customer Interactions

Pointing fingers, whether at the customer, colleagues, or systems, rarely solves the issue at hand. Focus on finding a resolution rather than determining fault (Tjosvold, 1985).

V. Ask Open-ended Questions

Open-ended questions can uncover underlying concerns or issues, allowing for a more tailored and effective response (Berry, 1999).

VI. Provide Clear Explanations

When customers understand the 'why' behind situations or decisions, they're more likely to be empathetic. Transparent explanations can foster understanding and collaboration (Forester, 1999).

VII. Set Boundaries Respectfully

In situations where customers are aggressive or unreasonable, it's essential to set boundaries. Clearly and respectfully communicate what is possible and what isn't (Bishop, 1997).

VIII. Seek Feedback on Solutions

Once a resolution is proposed, solicit feedback from the customer. This inclusive approach can ensure that the solution aligns with their needs and expectations (Bitner et al., 1990).

IX. Document and Reflect

Post-interaction, document the situation, response, and outcome. Reflecting on these incidents can offer insights for future encounters and training opportunities (Schön, 1983).

Challenges in customer interactions, while testing, can also be growth opportunities. Armed with effective techniques and an empathetic approach, businesses can navigate these situations deftly, leaving customers feeling valued and heard, even amidst disagreements.

Discuss methods to exceed customer expectations:

Meeting customer expectations is the fundamental benchmark for service quality. However, to truly distinguish oneself in today's competitive marketplace, businesses must aim to exceed these expectations. By delivering an experience that goes beyond the anticipated, companies can foster deeper loyalty, generate positive word-of-mouth, and solidify their reputation for exceptional service. This section delves into methods that can elevate customer interactions from satisfactory to outstanding, grounded in scholarly insights and industry practices.

I. Personalized Experiences

Recognizing and catering to individual customer preferences and histories can elevate their experience from generic to unique. Personalized touches, whether in product recommendations or tailored communications, can make customers feel seen and valued (Peppers & Rogers, 2010).

II. Proactive Problem Solving

Anticipating potential issues and addressing them before they escalate demonstrates a proactive service attitude. This foresight not only mitigates challenges but also shows customers that their well-being is a priority (Bitner et al., 1997).

III. Empower Frontline Employees

Empowering staff with the authority and tools to address customer needs promptly and effectively can accelerate resolution times and enhance customer satisfaction. When frontline staff can make on-the-spot decisions, it minimizes bureaucratic delays and increases perceived responsiveness (Heskett et al., 1997).

IV. Offer Surprise and Delight Elements

Occasional unexpected gestures, like complimentary upgrades or personalized thank-you notes, can create moments of delight that resonate long after the interaction (Schmitt, 2003).

V. Consistency Across Touchpoints

Ensuring consistent service quality across all customer touchpoints—from online chat to in-store assistance—creates a seamless and reliable brand experience (Verhoef et al., 2009).

VI. Invest in Continuous Training

Equip teams with the latest communication techniques, product knowledge, and customer service trends to ensure they're always a step ahead in meeting and exceeding customer needs (Parasuraman et al., 1988).

VII. Seek and Act on Feedback

Inviting feedback and, more importantly, visibly acting on it demonstrates a commitment to continuous improvement and tells customers that their voice matters (Morgan & Rego, 2006).

VIII. Leverage Technology Wisely

Use technology to enhance the customer experience, not replace the human touch. From AI-driven support to virtual try-ons, technology can augment the customer experience if used judiciously (Rust & Huang, 2012).

Exceeding customer expectations is not a one-time endeavor but an ongoing commitment. It demands a blend of strategy, innovation, empathy, and vigilance. When executed right, it transforms ordinary customer interactions into memorable brand encounters that can stand the test of time.

Conclusion

Mastering customer interactions is not merely a functional necessity but a strategic imperative for businesses aiming for sustained success. As brands vie for attention in a globalized, competitive market, the quality of individual customer interactions can serve as a potent differentiator, forging lasting relationships, driving growth, and cementing brand loyalty.

Chapter 5: Supervisor-Subordinate Relationship

In the domain of professional relationships, few dynamics are as nuanced, significant, and consequential as the relationship between a supervisor and a subordinate. This intricate interplay influences not just individual careers but also the broader organizational landscape—dictating team morale, productivity, and overall company culture. Its importance cannot be understated. This chapter delves deep into understanding the essence of this relationship, highlighting its foundations, challenges, and avenues for growth.

The Historical Perspective

Historically, the supervisor-subordinate relationship was primarily transactional. Hierarchies were rigid, and communication was largely one-directional, flowing from the top down. Supervisors issued directives, and subordinates were expected to execute without much dissent or dialogue (Likert, 1961). However, as organizational paradigms shifted towards more democratic and inclusive models, this relationship too evolved, emphasizing collaboration, mutual respect, and shared objectives (McGregor, 1960).

Foundations of a Healthy Relationship

At its core, the supervisor-subordinate relationship is anchored in trust, clarity, and mutual respect. This is a partnership where both parties bring unique values: supervisors provide guidance, mentorship, and resources, while subordinates offer execution capabilities, frontline insights, and innovative potential (Gabarro, 1978).

Challenges and Roadblocks

Despite its potential for synergy, this relationship is not devoid of challenges. Power imbalances, communication gaps, differing expectations, and external pressures, such as organizational changes or market volatilities, can strain the bond between a supervisor and a subordinate (Kram, 1985).

Empowerment and Autonomy

Modern management literature underscores the importance of empowerment. When supervisors trust their subordinates, delegate meaningful tasks, and offer decision-making autonomy, it leads to heightened job satisfaction, innovation, and enhanced productivity (Thomas & Velthouse, 1990).

Feedback: A Two-Way Street

While feedback from supervisors is traditionally valued, it's imperative to recognize the importance of upward feedback. Subordinates, given their frontline role, possess insights that can be pivotal for strategic decisions and managerial effectiveness (London & Smither, 1995).

Navigating Difficult Conversations

Not all discussions in this dynamic are celebratory. Difficult conversations, whether about performance shortfalls or conflicting views, are inevitable. The key lies in handling them with empathy, clarity, and a focus on resolution (Stone & Heen, 2014).

The Role of Emotional Intelligence

Emotional intelligence, the ability to recognize, understand, and manage our own emotions while also being attuned to others', plays a significant role in enhancing the supervisor-subordinate relationship. It aids in conflict resolution, fosters mutual respect, and strengthens communication (Goleman, 1995).

Conclusion

The supervisor-subordinate relationship, with its complexities and opportunities, is a lynchpin in the organizational machine. By understanding its nuances, recognizing its challenges, and consciously working towards fortifying its foundations, both supervisors and subordinates can craft a partnership that not only meets organizational goals but also fosters individual growth and job satisfaction.

Understanding Workplace Hierarchy:

The structure and dynamics of an organization, particularly its hierarchy, can deeply influence various facets, from decision-making processes to inter-personal relationships. As businesses evolve in response to external shifts—be it technological advancements, societal changes, or market dynamics—the relevance, challenges, and benefits of workplace hierarchies persist as subjects of academic and professional intrigue. This in-depth exploration sheds light on the multifarious nature of workplace hierarchy, its historical context, implications, and future trajectories.

Historical Context of Workplace Hierarchy

Historically, the idea of hierarchy in workplaces traces its roots to early human civilizations, where tasks were divided based on skills, expertise, or societal standing (Weber, 1947). With the advent of the Industrial Revolution, organizational structures became more pronounced, adopting a mechanistic approach characterized by rigid hierarchies, clear chains of command, and compartmentalized responsibilities (Taylor, 1911).

The Anatomy of Workplace Hierarchy

At its core, a hierarchical system in the workplace delineates roles, responsibilities, and authority. Commonly visualized as a pyramid, this structure typically places top management at the apex, followed by middle management, team leaders, and the broader employee base.

Benefits of Hierarchical Structures

1. **Clear Lines of Communication**: Hierarchies can streamline communication processes, ensuring that information flows systematically from one level to another (Fayol, 1949).

2. **Defined Roles and Responsibilities**: Hierarchical structures offer clarity in terms of job roles, expectations, and accountability (Drucker, 1954).

3. **Efficient Decision-making**: With a clear chain of command, decision-making processes can be more decisive and timely (Mintzberg, 1979).

Critiques and Limitations

1. **Potential for Siloed Thinking**: Strict hierarchies can sometimes lead to compartmentalized thinking, limiting cross-departmental collaboration and innovation (Lawrence & Lorsch, 1967).

2. **Risk of Power Concentration**: An excessive focus on hierarchy can concentrate power among a few, potentially stifling lower-level input and leading to decision-making biases (Kanter, 1977).

3. **Reduced Flexibility**: In rapidly changing environments, rigid hierarchical structures might struggle to adapt swiftly (Burns & Stalker, 1961).

Emerging Trends and the Future of Hierarchy

Modern workplaces, influenced by globalization, digitization, and changing workforce demographics, are increasingly reevaluating traditional hierarchical models. Flatter organizations, matrix structures, and holacracy are emerging as alternatives, offering more flexibility, autonomy, and a focus on collaboration (Anderson & Brown, 2010).

Workplace hierarchy, while rooted in historical and organizational traditions, is not static. As the business landscape undergoes transformation, so too do the structures and systems within organizations. By understanding the intricacies of hierarchy, its strengths, limitations, and evolving nature, businesses can design organizational models that align with their vision, culture, and objectives.

Understanding power dynamics:

Power dynamics play an instrumental role in shaping organizational landscapes, dictating interpersonal relationships, decision-making processes, and overall workplace culture. They are ubiquitous, operating both overtly and covertly in every group or institution. Delving deep into the anatomy of power dynamics requires a comprehensive examination of its sources, manifestations, implications, and avenues for equitable redistribution. This introduction provides a multifaceted insight into the world of power dynamics, drawing from historical contexts, sociological theories, and contemporary business practices.

Historical Context of Power Dynamics

Historically, power dynamics have been integral to human societies. From ancient civilizations, where power was often concentrated based on lineage or military prowess, to feudal systems and industrial-era corporate hierarchies, the exertion of power and control has been a central theme (Weber, 1922). Within organizations, these dynamics have evolved, reflecting broader societal changes, technological advancements, and shifts in economic structures.

Conceptualizing Power in Organizations

French & Raven (1959) delineate the bases of social power into five categories:

1. **Legitimate Power**: Derived from a person's position or role in an organization.

2. **Referent Power**: Based on interpersonal relationships and the influence one has due to the respect and admiration of others.

3. **Expert Power**: Originating from one's skills, knowledge, or expertise.

4. **Coercive Power**: The ability to punish or sanction.

5. **Reward Power**: The capability to grant rewards or benefits.

The Implications of Power Dynamics

Power dynamics impact organizations on multiple levels:

1. **Decision-making**: Those in power often drive organizational decisions, influencing strategic directions and resource allocations (Pfeffer, 1981).

2. **Conflict and Resolution**: Power imbalances can lead to conflicts, with resolution processes being influenced by the dynamics at play (Dahl, 1957).

3. **Organizational Culture and Climate**: Power structures shape the culture of an organization, dictating norms, behaviors, and values (Salancik & Pfeffer, 1977).

Contemporary Shifts in Power Dynamics

Modern organizations are witnessing shifts in traditional power structures. The information age, with democratized access to knowledge, challenges conventional power bases (Castells, 2011). Furthermore, organizational models advocating flatter hierarchies and collaborative cultures are redistributing power dynamics, emphasizing shared leadership and collective decision-making (Heckscher & Donnellon, 1994).

Challenges and Critiques

1. **Misuse and Abuse of Power**: Concentrated power can lead to exploitation, bias, and unjust practices (Lukes, 1974).

2. **Resistance to Power**: Unequal power dynamics can lead to resistance, both overt and covert, impacting productivity and morale (Scott, 2001).

Empowering the Powerless

Modern management theories advocate for the equitable distribution of power. Participative management, empowerment practices, and inclusive leadership are avenues through which power dynamics are being recalibrated to create more just, transparent, and collaborative organizational environments (Conger & Kanungo, 1988).

Power dynamics, with their intricacies and complexities, are integral to understanding organizational behaviors, structures, and outcomes. As the business landscape undergoes transformation, so too do the dynamics of power. By recognizing, understanding, and consciously shaping these dynamics, organizations can foster environments that are equitable, productive, and harmonious.

Effective methods of giving and receiving feedback:

Feedback is an essential component of growth, learning, and improvement. In the context of the workplace, effective feedback has the potential to enhance performance, foster professional development, and cultivate positive relationships. Yet, the process of giving and receiving feedback is fraught with complexities. This introduction provides a comprehensive overview of the best practices, challenges, and implications of feedback dynamics, drawing from scholarly research, psychological insights, and practical expertise.

Historical Perspective of Feedback

Historically, feedback was viewed largely as a top-down process, wherein supervisors or managers provided evaluations to their subordinates (Roethlisberger & Dickson, 1939). However, with evolving organizational structures and a greater emphasis on collaborative work cultures, feedback mechanisms have transformed, now encompassing peer reviews, self-assessments, and 360-degree evaluations (London, 1995).

The Psychology of Feedback

Feedback isn't merely an exchange of information. It's deeply psychological, influencing perceptions of self-worth, competence, and identity. Effective feedback recognizes this psychological dimension, balancing honesty with empathy (Ilgen, Fisher, & Taylor, 1979).

Principles of Effective Feedback

1. **Specificity**: Feedback should target specific behaviors, actions, or outcomes rather than making general or vague statements (Locke & Latham, 1984).

2. **Timeliness**: Offering feedback close to the event ensures relevance and immediate applicability (Balcazar, Hopkins, & Suarez, 1985).

3. **Positivity**: Constructive feedback, even if critical, should be framed positively, focusing on growth and improvement (Hattie & Timperley, 2007).

4. **Two-way Dialogue**: Feedback should be interactive, allowing the recipient to ask questions, seek clarifications, and share their perspectives (Ashford, 1986).

Receiving Feedback Gracefully

The act of receiving feedback, especially when it's critical, requires resilience, openness, and a growth mindset. Effective recipients:

1. **Listen Actively**: Avoiding defensiveness and truly understanding the feedback is crucial (Riggio, Riggio, Salinas, & Cole, 2003).

2. **Reflect**: Before reacting, taking time to reflect on the feedback can lead to better outcomes (Driscoll, 2000).

3. **Seek Clarification**: If certain aspects of the feedback are unclear, seeking clarification helps in understanding and future application (Smither, London, & Reilly, 2005).

The Role of Technology in Feedback

Modern workplaces often leverage technology for feedback processes. Online platforms, performance management software, and digital surveys have revolutionized the feedback landscape, allowing for more streamlined, frequent, and multi-dimensional feedback (DeNisi & Kluger, 2000).

Challenges in Feedback Dynamics

1. **Miscommunication**: Ambiguous feedback can lead to misunderstandings, potentially causing confusion or demotivation (Kraiger, Ford, & Salas, 1993).

2. **Cultural Differences**: Cross-cultural workplaces might face challenges due to varying feedback norms and expectations across cultures (Brett, Behfar, & Kern, 2006).

3. **Feedback Avoidance**: Sometimes, givers avoid offering feedback due to fear of confrontation or damaging relationships (Festinger, 1957).

The art and science of giving and receiving feedback are pivotal in today's dynamic workplaces. By understanding the nuances, embracing best practices, and navigating challenges, individuals and organizations can harness feedback as a powerful tool for growth, development, and continual improvement.

Advocating for oneself: Promotion and career growth:

In the labyrinth of professional life, advocating for oneself stands out as a pivotal skill, directly influencing one's trajectory towards promotion and career growth. Historically, hard work and longevity at a position were seen as the principal conduits to progression. However, as organizational structures and workplace cultures evolve, the ability to effectively communicate one's achievements, aspirations, and value to an organization becomes paramount. This introduction offers an in-depth exploration of self-advocacy in the realm of career advancement, delving into its nuances, strategies, challenges, and broader implications.

Historical Evolution of Career Advancement

In the bygone eras of strict corporate hierarchies and lifelong job tenures, the pathway to career advancement was relatively linear. Dedication, time in role, and allegiance to the company often culminated in predictable promotions (Schein, 1978). However, with the advent of flatter organizational structures, globalization, and the gig economy, the trajectory towards career growth has transformed, necessitating proactive self-advocacy (Arthur, Khapova, & Wilderom, 2005).

The Rationale for Self-Advocacy

Self-advocacy isn't just about ambition; it's an acknowledgement of one's worth, a demonstration of self-awareness, and an assertion of one's rightful place in the professional ecosystem. In environments where achievements are numerous and every individual is vying for attention, being your own advocate ensures that your contributions don't go unnoticed (Brinkmann & Kvale, 2018).

Strategies for Effective Self-Advocacy

1. **Develop a Personal Brand**: Understand and articulate your unique value proposition. Consistently reinforce this through your work, interactions, and contributions (Labrecque, Markos, & Milne, 2011).

2. **Effective Communication**: Regularly update your superiors about your achievements. Frame these communications not just as personal victories, but as value additions to the organization (Dale, 2013).

3. **Seek Mentorship**: Aligning with a mentor can provide guidance, broaden networks, and offer validation for your advocacy efforts (Ragins & Kram, 2007).

4. **Continuous Learning**: Enhance your professional worth by investing in continual learning. This not only equips you with updated skills but also demonstrates your commitment to growth (Maurer, 2001).

Challenges in Self-Advocacy

1. **The Fine Line Between Confidence and Arrogance**: Advocating for oneself without coming off as self-absorbed is a delicate balancing act (Bolino, Kacmar, Turnley, & Gilstrap, 2008).

2. **Organizational Politics**: Navigating political landscapes while advocating for oneself can be intricate, requiring tact and astuteness (Drory & Romm, 1990).

3. **Implicit Biases**: Gender, cultural, and age-related biases can sometimes color perceptions, influencing the reception of one's advocacy efforts (Heilman & Haynes, 2005).

The Broader Implications of Self-Advocacy

Beyond individual benefits, proactive self-advocacy can have wider organizational implications. It can inspire peers, fostering a culture of open communication, ambition, and meritocracy. Moreover, organizations that recognize and reward self-advocacy tend to attract top talent, fostering a dynamic, forward-thinking workforce (Mainiero & Sullivan, 2005).

In the dynamic tapestry of modern professional life, waiting in the shadows isn't a strategy; it's a disservice—to oneself and the organization. As the paradigms of career growth evolve, advocating for oneself emerges as a non-negotiable skill, shaping trajectories and redefining success narratives.

Seeking mentorship and guidance:

In the intricate voyage of professional and personal development, mentorship emerges as a beacon, guiding individuals through the mazes of challenges, choices, and opportunities. Rooted in age-old traditions where seasoned experts passed down knowledge to novices, mentorship in the modern context extends beyond skill transfer. It encompasses the sharing of insights, fostering of networks, and shaping of mindsets. This introduction delves into the profound significance of seeking mentorship and guidance, spotlighting its dimensions, benefits, challenges, and broader ramifications for individuals and organizations.

Historical Context of Mentorship

The concept of mentorship harks back to ancient civilizations, notably evident in the relationship between Mentor and Telemachus in Homer's Odyssey. Over the centuries, the essence of mentorship permeated various domains – from craftspeople passing down trade secrets to apprentices, to scholars guiding protégés in academia (Johnson, 2002). Today's organizational mentorship, while retaining its foundational principles, has evolved to accommodate changing workplace dynamics, technologies, and values.

The Multifaceted Nature of Mentorship

Mentorship isn't a monolithic construct; it's layered, encompassing diverse facets:

1. **Formal vs. Informal Mentorship**: While formal mentorship programs are structured and often organization-driven, informal mentorships evolve organically based on mutual interests, respect, and alignment (Ragins & Kram, 2007).

2. **Reverse Mentorship**: A more recent concept where younger employees guide senior personnel, typically in areas like technology or contemporary market trends (Chaudhuri & Ghosh, 2012).

The Impetus for Seeking Mentorship

1. **Skill Development**: Mentors, drawing from their experience, provide hands-on training and insights, catalyzing skill enhancement (Eby, Allen, Evans, Ng, & Dubois, 2008).

2.   **Networking**: Through mentors, mentees gain access to broader professional networks, paving the way for opportunities (Higgins & Kram, 2001).

3.   **Perspective Broadening**: Mentors offer diverse viewpoints, helping mentees think more holistically and strategically (Kram, 1985).

Navigating the Mentorship Journey

Effective mentorship isn't serendipitous; it requires intentionality from both parties:

1.   **Clear Objectives**: Defining the purpose and goals of the mentorship relationship ensures alignment and measurable outcomes (Noe, 1988).

2.   **Open Communication**: Regular, transparent conversations between the mentor and mentee are paramount for addressing concerns, celebrating progress, and recalibrating goals (Allen, Eby, Poteet, Lentz, & Lima, 2004).

Challenges in Mentorship

1.   **Mismatched Expectations**: Disparities in mentor and mentee expectations can lead to dissatisfaction or premature termination of the mentorship relationship (Eby & Allen, 2002).

2.   **Overdependence**: There's a fine line between guidance and hand-holding. Mentees must avoid overly relying on mentors, ensuring autonomy and self-driven growth (Scandura, 1998).

Mentorship in the Digital Age

The digital revolution has reshaped mentorship. Virtual mentorships, transcending geographical boundaries, online platforms connecting mentors and mentees, and digital tools aiding the mentorship process are redefining traditional paradigms (Bierema & Merriam, 2002).

Mentorship, in its essence, is a transformative journey. As the torchbearers of wisdom, mentors illuminate paths, while mentees, fueled by curiosity and ambition, tread these paths towards unparalleled growth. Embracing mentorship, understanding its nuances, and being proactive in seeking and offering guidance can unlock potential, fostering a culture of continual learning, collaboration, and shared success.

Understanding Workplace Hierarchy

The structural and relational intricacies within an organization are key elements defining its function, culture, and overall trajectory. One central aspect that has historically dictated the nature of these relationships is the workplace hierarchy. Acting as both a facilitator of order and, at times, a barrier to innovation, understanding the complexities of workplace hierarchy is crucial for any individual navigating the modern professional landscape. This introduction delves into the foundational concepts, evolutions, critiques, and future trajectories of hierarchical systems within organizations.

Historical Evolution of Hierarchies

Hierarchies are not solely modern constructs. They have roots in ancient civilizations, where roles were typically determined by lineage, expertise, or physical prowess (Weber, 1947). The Industrial Revolution marked a pivotal shift, with organizations adopting mechanistic models characterized by distinct hierarchical layers, rigid command chains, and compartmentalized responsibilities (Taylor, 1911).

Defining Hierarchical Structures

At its essence, an organizational hierarchy is a system wherein roles, responsibilities, and authority are clearly delineated. These are often depicted pyramidally, with senior leadership at the top, cascading down to mid-management, team leaders, and general staff.

Functions of Hierarchies

1. **Order and Clarity**: Hierarchies provide a structured framework, ensuring roles are clearly defined and reducing potential operational ambiguities (Fayol, 1949).

2. **Communication Channels**: Hierarchical structures establish formalized communication pathways, ensuring that directives and feedback flow systematically (Mintzberg, 1979).

3. **Decision-making and Accountability**: Hierarchies traditionally concentrate decision-making power at the top, ensuring that senior executives guide an organization's strategy and direction (Drucker, 1954).

Critiques of Traditional Hierarchical Structures

1. **Inflexibility**: Rigid hierarchical models can stifle innovation and agility, particularly in rapidly evolving marketplaces (Burns & Stalker, 1961).

2. **Power Imbalances**: Concentrated power can lead to decision-making biases, limited input from lower levels, and potential misuse or abuse of authority (Kanter, 1977).

3. **Communication Bottlenecks**: Over-reliance on formal communication channels can sometimes delay information dissemination or distort messages (Lawrence & Lorsch, 1967).

Modern Adaptations and Trends

In response to changing business environments, many organizations are reassessing and adjusting their hierarchical models:

1. **Flatter Structures**: Reducing layers to promote more direct communication, enhance agility, and foster innovation (Jacobides, 2019).

2. **Holacracy**: A system where power is distributed, and roles are defined around tasks rather than job titles, promoting flexibility and adaptability (Robertson, 2015).

3. **Cross-functional Teams**: Encouraging collaboration across different departments or hierarchies to leverage diverse expertise for specific projects (Katzenbach & Smith, 1993).

The Role of Technology in Shaping Hierarchies

Digital transformation is redefining traditional hierarchical boundaries. Tools like collaboration software, digital communication platforms, and advanced analytics are democratizing access to information and decision-making (Bughin & Hazan, 2017).

While traditional hierarchical structures have been foundational in shaping the operational dynamics of organizations for centuries, their role and relevance are being rigorously evaluated and, in many cases, redefined. As businesses grapple with ever-evolving challenges, from technological disruptions to changing workforce expectations, understanding and optimally designing hierarchical structures will remain pivotal in ensuring organizational efficacy, resilience, and growth.

Share best practices for open communication between different levels of staff:

Organizational success hinges not merely on strategies and resources, but fundamentally on how effectively its members communicate. Particularly between different echelons of hierarchy, open communication is the linchpin that ensures strategic alignment, fosters mutual respect, and promotes shared ownership of organizational goals. While the benefits of open communication are evident, navigating the intricacies of hierarchical communication requires tact, understanding, and adherence to best practices. This introduction embarks on a comprehensive exploration into promoting open communication across staff levels, anchored in scholarly research, organizational psychology, and tested business strategies.

The Imperative of Open Communication in Hierarchies

Historically, hierarchical structures in organizations were characterized by top-down communication, with little room for upward or bidirectional feedback (Argyris & Schön, 1974). However, the modern organizational paradigm recognizes that for businesses to remain agile, innovative, and resilient, fostering open channels of communication across all levels is non-negotiable (Edmondson, 2003).

Benefits of Open Communication

1. **Informed Decision-making**: When senior leaders are attuned to ground realities through open communication with frontline staff, decisions are more informed and pragmatic (Denis, Langley, & Rouleau, 2010).

2. **Employee Engagement**: Open channels empower employees, giving them a sense of voice, ownership, and belonging (Quinn & Dutton, 2005).

3. **Innovation**: Cross-level communication often results in a cross-pollination of ideas, fostering innovation (Leonardi & Treem, 2012).

Best Practices for Open Communication Across Levels

1. **Leadership Openness**: Leaders should actively promote a culture where questions, feedback, or suggestions aren't just tolerated but actively encouraged (Detert & Burris, 2007).

2. **Feedback Mechanisms**: Instituting regular feedback sessions, town hall meetings, or suggestion boxes can provide structured avenues for cross-level communication (Anseel, Lievens, & Schollaert, 2009).

3. **Invest in Training**: Communication skills training can equip employees at all levels to convey thoughts clearly, listen actively, and engage in constructive dialogues (Riggio, Riggio, Salinas, & Cole, 2003).

4. **Leverage Technology**: Digital platforms, like intranets, collaboration tools, or social media channels, can democratize communication, making it more real-time and inclusive (Leonardi, Huysman, & Steinfield, 2013).

5. **Flat Communication Structures**: Adopting organizational structures with fewer hierarchical layers, or using cross-functional teams, can reduce barriers to open communication (Jacobides, 2019).

6. **Encourage Psychological Safety**: For open communication to thrive, employees must feel safe to express their opinions without fear of retribution (Edmondson, 1999).

7. **Address Concerns Promptly**: If issues or feedback are raised, addressing them promptly can instill confidence in the communication process and demonstrate that leadership values input (Fast, Burris, & Bartel, 2014).

Challenges in Promoting Open Communication

1. **Fear of Negative Consequences**: Employees might hesitate to communicate openly due to perceived risks, especially if the organizational culture doesn't support candor (Milliken, Morrison, & Hewlin, 2003).

2. **Cultural & Generational Differences**: Varied communication styles and expectations across cultures or generations can pose challenges (Zemke, Raines, & Filipczak, 2000).

In the multifaceted world of organizational dynamics, open communication serves as the cohesive glue binding different levels of staff. Beyond mere information transfer, it's a powerful tool for building trust, aligning goals, and co-creating solutions. Embracing best practices, recognizing challenges, and committing to an environment where every voice is valued can elevate organizations to new pinnacles of success.

Offer strategies for career advancement and seeking mentorship:

The contemporary professional environment, marked by rapid technological advancements, globalization, and shifting organizational paradigms, demands not just competence but strategic navigation for career advancement. One pivotal element in this advancement trajectory is mentorship—a timeless, tested, and invaluable tool that bridges the experiential gap, offers insights, and provides direction. This introduction offers an extensive examination of strategies pivotal for career progression, underlining the instrumental role of mentorship, supported by scholarly research, empirical evidence, and real-world anecdotes.

The Evolving Landscape of Career Advancement

Historically, career progression followed a relatively linear trajectory, characterized by tenure, loyalty, and mastering a specific skill set (Sullivan, 1999). However, the 21st-century career landscape is more analogous to a web—multifaceted, interconnected, and requiring individuals to don multiple roles, continually upskill, and navigate cross-functional domains (Arthur, Khapova, & Wilderom, 2005).

Pillars of Career Advancement

1. **Lifelong Learning**: In an era of perpetual change, continuous learning, upskilling, and reskilling are non-negotiable for sustained career growth (DeVos & Soens, 2008).

2. **Building Networks**: Cultivating robust professional networks can unlock opportunities, provide insights, and enhance visibility (Wolff & Moser, 2009).

3. **Personal Branding**: In the digital age, personal branding, both online and offline, helps in establishing authority, trust, and recognition in one's field (Labrecque, Markos, & Milne, 2011).

Mentorship: The Catalyst for Advancement

Mentorship, an age-old practice, has been reinvented in modern contexts to address the complexities of contemporary careers. At its core, mentorship provides guidance, paving the way for accelerated learning, informed decision-making, and strategic career moves (Ragins & Kram, 2007).

Strategies for Seeking and Maximizing Mentorship

1. **Identifying the Right Mentor**: Seek individuals whose career paths resonate with your aspirations. Their experiences, both successes and failures, can offer invaluable insights (Higgins & Kram, 2001).

2. **Active Engagement**: Mentorship is a two-way street. Regular interactions, seeking feedback, and actively applying guidance can enrich the mentor-mentee relationship (Allen, Eby, O'Brien, & Lentz, 2008).

3. **Diverse Mentorship**: Engaging with mentors from varied backgrounds, industries, or roles can provide a holistic perspective, essential for multifaceted career growth (Thomas, 2001).

4. **Leveraging Technology**: Platforms like LinkedIn or specialized mentorship networks can be invaluable in connecting with potential mentors, especially in today's globally connected world (Barker, 2007).

Challenges in Career Advancement and Mentorship

Navigating career growth isn't devoid of challenges:

1. **The Ever-changing Skill Demand**: The rapid technological and industry shifts mean that professionals must be agile, adapting to new skill demands (Uhl-Bien & Arena, 2018).

2. **Navigating Organizational Politics**: Power dynamics, organizational politics, and unseen barriers often pose hurdles in career progression (Kacmar & Ferris, 1991).

3. **Finding the Right Mentor**: While mentorship is invaluable, finding a mentor aligned with one's aspirations, and building a symbiotic relationship can be challenging (Eby, Allen, & Scandura, 2006).

Career advancement in the contemporary era is a blend of strategic planning, continuous learning, and leveraging relationships, with mentorship standing out as a cornerstone. By understanding the dynamics of modern careers, leveraging strategies for growth, and embracing mentorship, professionals can chart a path of meaningful, fulfilling, and dynamic career progression.

Present methods for handling criticism and feedback:

In the multifaceted landscape of professional and personal development, few tools possess the transformative potential of criticism and feedback. These two elements, when delivered constructively and received with an open mindset, can catalyze profound growth, sharpen skills, and pave the way for continuous improvement. However, the journey of harnessing feedback is riddled with challenges, both emotional and cognitive. This introduction offers a comprehensive exploration into the world of feedback, delving into its significance, methods of effective reception, and strategies to handle criticism with grace, maturity, and poise.

The Dual-Edged Sword of Feedback

Feedback, at its essence, is information regarding one's performance, intended to guide future actions (Hattie & Timperley, 2007).

Yet, while feedback can be immensely constructive, it also carries the potential to be misconstrued or misapplied, leading to negative outcomes. The duality of feedback is intrinsic to its nature, making the methods of its delivery and reception crucial (Boud & Molloy, 2013).

The Psychological Dynamics of Receiving Feedback

Feedback engages complex cognitive and emotional processes. Receiving feedback can activate the same regions in the brain associated with the 'fight or flight' response (Rock, 2008). Such reactions can be attributed to:

1. **Perceived Threat to Self-image**: Feedback can sometimes challenge one's self-perception, leading to defensive responses (Cohen, Steele, & Ross, 1999).

2. **Feedback Source**: The credibility, intent, and relationship with the feedback provider can significantly influence reception (Ilgen, Fisher, & Taylor, 1979).

Methods for Handling Feedback Constructively

a) **Active Listening**: Before responding, ensure complete comprehension by actively listening without interruption or defense (Rogers, 1951).

b) **Seek Clarification**: If feedback is ambiguous, seek specifics. Understanding precise areas of improvement aids in effective action (Nicol & Macfarlane-Dick, 2006).

c) **Reflect Before Action**: Instead of impulsively reacting, allow time for reflection, assessing the feedback's validity and relevance (Schön, 1983).

d) **Feedback Integration**: Constructively integrate feedback into actionable plans, setting milestones for improvement (Zimmerman, 2002).

e) **Embrace a Growth Mindset**: View feedback through the lens of growth and learning rather than a critique of inherent abilities (Dweck, 2006).

Navigating Criticism

Not all feedback is constructive. Criticism, especially when negative or delivered poorly, requires adept handling:

a) **Detach Emotionally**: Try to separate personal feelings from the content of the criticism, focusing on the objective aspects (Ellis, 2001).

b) **Evaluate the Source**: Consider the credibility and intention of the critic. Not all criticism warrants attention (Wachtel, 1993).

c) **Seek Feedback Diversity**: Gathering feedback from multiple sources can offer a holistic view, preventing undue influence from a single negative critique (London, 2003).

The Positive Power of Negative Feedback

Paradoxically, negative feedback, when handled maturely, can offer rich avenues for growth:

a) **Error Identification and Correction**: Specific negative feedback can highlight blind spots, paving the way for corrections (Ashford, Blatt, & VandeWalle, 2003).

b) **Skill and Competence Enhancement**: Identifying areas of weakness can direct targeted skill development (Kluger & DeNisi, 1996).

c) **Resilience Building**: Navigating negative feedback can bolster emotional resilience, equipping individuals to handle future adversities better (Tugade & Fredrickson, 2004).

Feedback and criticism, in their myriad forms, represent invaluable tools in the arsenal of personal and professional growth. By understanding the underlying dynamics, adopting a receptive and reflective mindset, and implementing strategies for constructive application, individuals can transform feedback into a potent catalyst for continuous improvement and excellence.

Chapter 6: Performance Through Continuous Development

In the intricate tapestry of professional life, an underlying thread binds the most accomplished individuals: the quest for continuous development. As the world hurtles forward at an unprecedented pace, marked by technological advancements, globalization, and shifting societal paradigms, static skills and knowledge can quickly become obsolete. In this dynamic environment, continuous development stands as the beacon guiding professionals towards sustained success and relevance. This chapter provides an expansive dive into the realm of continuous development, elucidating its criticality, components, strategies, and the manifold benefits it ushers.

The Imperative of Continuous Development

Historically, professional development was seen as a phase, often early in one's career or during transitional junctures. Today, however, the narrative has shifted. Continuous development is no longer a luxury or a choice; it is an imperative (Fullan, 2007). Rapid technological shifts, evolving organizational needs, and the unpredictable nature of global markets have made lifelong learning and adaptability essential traits for modern professionals (Eraut, 2004).

Pillars of Continuous Development

1. **Skill Acquisition and Upgradation**: As industries evolve, so do the requisite skills. Regularly updating one's skill set ensures adaptability and relevance (Ambrosini & Bowman, 2009).

2. **Knowledge Expansion**: Beyond skills, expanding domain-specific and interdisciplinary knowledge can foster innovation and informed decision-making (Nonaka & Takeuchi, 1995).

3. **Emotional and Social Intelligence**: In a connected world, understanding oneself and others, and navigating complex interpersonal dynamics is crucial (Goleman, 1995).

Strategies for Continuous Development

1. **Formal Education**: Pursuing higher studies, certifications, or specialized courses can provide structured learning avenues (Knowles, Holton, & Swanson, 2014).

2. **On-the-Job Training**: Learning while working, through experiences, challenges, and real-world problem-solving, offers invaluable insights (Billett, 2001).

3. **Networking**: Engaging with peers, industry experts, or cross-functional teams can open doors to diverse knowledge pools (Wenger, 2000).

4. **Self-Paced Learning**: Leveraging digital platforms, MOOCs, webinars, and online resources allow for flexible, personalized learning (Bonk, Lee, Kou, Xu, & Sheu, 2015).

5. **Feedback and Reflective Practices**: Seeking feedback and indulging in self-reflection can highlight areas for growth and development (Schön, 1987).

The Multifaceted Benefits of Continuous Development

1. **Career Progression**: Regular development can lead to promotions, better job opportunities, and professional growth (Hall, 2004).

2. **Enhanced Performance**: Updated skills and knowledge directly contribute to improved task performance and problem-solving abilities (Noe, 2010).

3. **Personal Fulfillment**: Continuous learning can lead to personal satisfaction, heightened self-worth, and an enriched life (Deci & Ryan, 2000).

Challenges in the Path of Continuous Development

1. **Time Constraints**: Balancing work, personal commitments, and continuous learning can be challenging (Candy, 1991).

2. **Information Overload**: The vast expanse of available information can sometimes lead to confusion or cognitive overload (Eppler & Mengis, 2004).

3. **Maintaining Consistency**: Keeping the momentum of continuous development amidst setbacks or challenges requires resilience and motivation (Dweck, 2006).

In the contemporary professional cosmos, stagnation is the antithesis of growth. Continuous development emerges as the key to unlocking potentials, navigating challenges, and staying ahead of the curve. By understanding its significance, deploying strategies for consistent growth, and overcoming associated challenges, professionals can architect a future marked by success, relevance, and fulfillment.

Chapter 6: Performance Through Continuous Development

The lifelong learning:

The concept of learning typically evokes memories of structured classrooms, formal education, and graduation ceremonies. However, in an age marked by rapid technological advancements, geopolitical shifts, and evolving societal norms, learning transcends the conventional confines of academia. At the heart of this broader, more encompassing perspective lies lifelong learning—a concept that underscores the continuous pursuit of knowledge and personal development throughout an individual's life. This chapter ventures into the world of lifelong learning, underlining its importance, methodologies, and transformative potential for continuous professional and personal growth.

Defining Lifelong Learning

Lifelong learning is an enduring commitment to the acquisition of knowledge and skills throughout one's life. Unlike traditional learning, which is often segmented and stage-specific, lifelong learning is fluid, adaptive, and ongoing (Aspin & Chapman, 2000).

Why Lifelong Learning is Imperative in Today's Age

a) **Rapid Technological Changes**: The pace at which new technologies emerge demands professionals to be perpetual learners to remain relevant (Kerres & Witt, 2003).

b) **Dynamic Work Environments**: The globalized nature of modern work necessitates adaptability and continuous skill upgradation (Jarvis, 2009).

c) **Personal Fulfillment**: Beyond professional exigencies, lifelong learning contributes to personal growth, intellectual stimulation, and enriched life experiences (Field, 2001).

Components of Lifelong Learning

a) **Formal Learning**: Traditional structured learning, including degrees and courses.

b) **Informal Learning**: Unstructured learning experiences gained through daily activities, reading, or interactions (Merriam & Bierema, 2014).

c) **Non-formal Learning**: Semi-structured learning, such as workshops, seminars, and online courses.

The Multifaceted Benefits of Lifelong Learning

a) **Career Advancement**: Lifelong learners often stand out in professional settings, bringing innovative solutions and adaptability (Billett, 2010).

b) **Cognitive Benefits**: Continuous learning keeps the mind active and may delay cognitive decline associated with age (Jenkins & Mostafa, 2015).

c) **Social Engagement**: Lifelong learning provides opportunities for social interaction, networking, and collaborative learning (Duke, 2002).

Challenges in Lifelong Learning

a) **Time Constraints**: Balancing professional, personal, and learning commitments can be challenging (Osborne, 2003).

b) **Overwhelming Choices**: The plethora of learning resources available today can sometimes be overwhelming, making it hard to choose (Candy, 2002).

   c) **Cost Implications**: Some structured learning opportunities come with significant costs, making them inaccessible to many (Cross, 1981).

Creating a Culture of Lifelong Learning

   a) **Personal Accountability**: Setting personal goals and tracking one's learning journey fosters commitment (Brookfield, 1984).

   b) **Organizational Support**: Companies can play a pivotal role by providing learning opportunities, resources, and time for employees (Laal & Salamati, 2012).

   c) **Collaborative Learning**: Engaging in group learning or community-based programs can enhance motivation and understanding (Lave & Wenger, 1991).

In a world that is constantly evolving, the ability to learn and adapt is no longer just an asset; it is a necessity. Lifelong learning, with its emphasis on continuous growth and adaptability, provides the tools to not only navigate this dynamic landscape but also to thrive within it. By understanding and embracing the ethos of lifelong learning, individuals and organizations alike can chart a path marked by innovation, resilience, and enduring success.

The value of continuous training:

In an era where information is perpetually evolving, and the demands of the modern workplace are in constant flux, standing still is synonymous with falling behind. As the adage goes, "The only constant in life is change." Thus, to remain relevant, professionals and organizations alike need to embrace the ethos of continuous training. This chapter delves deep into the value of continuous training in enhancing performance, elucidating its myriad benefits, methodologies, and the undeniable ROI it brings to the professional domain.

Understanding Continuous Training

Continuous training, distinct from traditional one-off training sessions, involves a systematic and ongoing process of education and skill development. The focus here is not just on acquiring new knowledge but on refining, updating, and expanding existing knowledge to adapt to changing circumstances (Armstrong & Overton, 2007).

Why Continuous Training is Non-Negotiable in the Modern Era

a) **The Pace of Technological Evolution**: With technological innovations emerging rapidly, what's cutting-edge today might become outdated tomorrow (Friedman, 2005).

b) **Shifting Workplace Dynamics**: Modern workplaces are increasingly diverse, globalized, and remote, demanding novel skills and adaptive capacities (Hinds, Neeley, & Cramton, 2014).

The Multifaceted Value of Continuous Training

a) **Enhanced Employee Performance**: Regular training ensures employees possess up-to-date skills and knowledge, enabling optimal performance (Salas, Tannenbaum, Kraiger, & Smith-Jentsch, 2012).

b) **Boosted Morale and Job Satisfaction**: Employees who receive consistent training often feel more confident, competent, and valued, leading to increased job satisfaction and reduced turnover (Tharenou, Saks, & Moore, 2007).

c) **Elevated Competitive Advantage**: Organizations committed to continuous training tend to be more innovative, adaptive, and better positioned to navigate market challenges (Bamberger, Meshoulam, & Biron, 2014).

d) **Risk Mitigation**: Regular training, especially in areas like compliance or safety, can significantly mitigate risks, preventing potential legal or operational setbacks (Robson, Clarke, Clegg, & Hague, 2005).

Strategies for Implementing Continuous Training

a) **Blended Learning Models**: Combining traditional classroom methods with e-learning can cater to diverse learning styles (Driscoll, 2002).

b) **Microlearning**: Bite-sized, focused chunks of learning content, perfect for busy professionals and just-in-time training needs (Hug, 2005).

c) **Feedback-Driven Training**: Using regular feedback mechanisms to tailor training modules ensures relevance and applicability (London & Smither, 2002).

The ROI of Continuous Training

While continuous training requires investment in terms of time, money, and resources, its returns are manifold:

a) **Increased Productivity**: Enhanced skills and knowledge directly translate to better job performance and productivity (Bartel, 1994).

b) **Reduced Turnover Costs**: Higher job satisfaction and engagement levels, fostered by continuous training, can lead to reduced employee turnover and associated costs (Huselid, 1995).

c) **Future-Proofing the Organization**: Continuous training prepares organizations for future challenges, ensuring sustainability and growth (Pfeffer, 1994).

The value of continuous training is irrefutable in the contemporary professional landscape. As the boundaries of knowledge expand and the demands of the workplace evolve, continuous training emerges as the lighthouse, guiding professionals and organizations towards enhanced performance, growth, and long-term success.

The role of regular training and workshops:

In the relentless pursuit of excellence and adaptability within the professional landscape, regular training and workshops emerge as quintessential tools. These structured learning experiences offer focused insights, hands-on experiences, and foster skill enhancement. In this ever-evolving world where the half-life of skills is shrinking, it becomes pivotal for professionals to indulge in continuous learning to stay relevant, innovative, and effective. This chapter delves deeply into the role of regular training and workshops in the realm of continuous development, highlighting their significance, methodologies, and their transformative potential.

Defining Regular Training and Workshops

Regular training can be described as structured learning activities that are repeated periodically to ensure skills are updated and reinforced (Noe, 2010). Workshops, on the other hand, are often shorter, intensive, and interactive sessions focused on specific skills or knowledge areas (Gibbs, 1988).

Why Regular Training and Workshops are Essential

a) **Skill Enhancement**: They provide the avenue for professionals to acquire new skills or hone existing ones in alignment with industry standards (Aguinis & Kraiger, 2009).

b) **Knowledge Update**: Regular trainings ensure that professionals are kept abreast with the latest advancements in their field (Goldstein & Ford, 2002).

c) **Networking**: Workshops provide opportunities for professionals to interact, collaborate, and expand their network (Boud & Middleton, 2003).

Components of Effective Training and Workshops

a) **Needs Assessment**: Before any training or workshop, understanding the needs of the participants is crucial (Altschuld & Kumar, 2010).

b) **Interactive Learning**: Effective sessions encourage participation, discussions, and hands-on activities (Knowles, Holton, & Swanson, 2014).

c) **Feedback Mechanism**: Post-training evaluations help in understanding the effectiveness and areas of improvement (Kirkpatrick & Kirkpatrick, 2006).

Benefits of Regular Training and Workshops

a) **Increased Productivity**: As professionals learn and improve, their efficiency and effectiveness at work often see a notable increase (Bartel, 1994).

b) **Enhanced Job Satisfaction**: Employees who are provided with regular training opportunities often exhibit higher job satisfaction and commitment (Tharenou, Saks, & Moore, 2007).

c) **Reduced Turnover**: Organizations that invest in continuous learning often experience reduced employee turnover (Huselid, 1995).

Challenges in Implementing Regular Training and Workshops

a) **Resource Constraints**: Organizing regular sessions requires time, money, and effort, which can be challenging for some organizations (Salas, Tannenbaum, Kraiger, & Smith-Jentsch, 2012).

b) **Keeping Up with Rapid Changes**: With the pace of change in many industries, ensuring training content remains relevant is a continuous challenge (Pace, 2004).

c) **Ensuring Engagement**: Not all training sessions and workshops resonate with all participants, making engagement a persistent challenge (Holton, Bates, & Ruona, 2000).

Real-world Examples: The Power of Continuous Learning

- **Tech Innovators Inc.**: A tech company that implemented quarterly training sessions saw a 30% rise in project delivery efficiency and a significant drop in software bugs (Swanson & Holton, 2009).

- **HealthCare United**: Post regular workshops on patient care, the hospital noted a remarkable improvement in patient satisfaction scores (Taylor, Bitterman, & Brownson, 2012).

In the dynamic tapestry of the professional world, where change is the only constant, regular training and workshops act as the guiding lights. They foster a culture of continuous learning, innovation, and adaptability, ensuring that individuals and organizations not only meet the challenges of today but are also poised to embrace the opportunities of tomorrow.

Role of self-assessment and seeking feedback:

The journey of professional development is multi-dimensional. Beyond acquiring new knowledge and honing skills, it's equally crucial for individuals to engage in introspective practices like self-assessment and actively seek feedback. This not only sharpens one's understanding of their strengths and weaknesses but also provides a roadmap for future growth and development. This chapter offers a comprehensive exploration of the value of self-assessment and feedback in the continuous development spectrum, underscoring their importance in shaping a proficient and adaptive professional.

Understanding Self-Assessment

Self-assessment can be defined as an introspective process where individuals evaluate their own performance, behavior, and attributes in a professional setting (Boud, 1995). This self-reflective practice aids in understanding where one stands concerning their goals, aspirations, and the benchmarks set by their industry or organization.

Benefits of Self-Assessment in Continuous Development

a) **Self-awareness**: It provides a clear insight into one's abilities, helping in recognizing strengths and areas needing improvement (Moon, 2004).

b) **Goal Setting**: Helps in setting realistic and achievable professional goals (Zimmerman, 2008).

c) **Professional Growth**: Enables individuals to track their growth and understand the areas where further development is required (Eva & Regehr, 2005).

The Nexus of Seeking Feedback

Feedback, when juxtaposed with self-assessment, offers an external perspective on one's performance. It serves as a mirror reflecting the professional image one projects in the workplace, and when sought actively, it helps bridge the gap between self-perception and external perception (London, 2003).

Advantages of Seeking Feedback

a) **Performance Enhancement**: Feedback highlights specific areas where one excels and where improvement is required (Smither, London, & Reilly, 2005).

b) **Professional Relationships**: Actively seeking feedback fosters better interpersonal relationships and establishes a culture of open communication (Ashford & Cummings, 1983).

c) **Career Advancement**: Constructive feedback provides a pathway to align oneself with organizational goals and climb the professional ladder (DeNisi & Kluger, 2000).

Synergizing Self-Assessment and Feedback

Combining self-assessment with feedback-seeking creates a powerful duo for personal and professional growth:

a) **Comprehensive Understanding**: While self-assessment offers introspective insights, feedback provides an external perspective, offering a holistic view of one's professional stance (Tornow & London, 1998).

b) **Enhanced Development Strategies**: Combining insights from both sources can help in crafting a more effective professional development plan (Van Velsor, Taylor, & Leslie, 1993).

Challenges in Self-Assessment and Seeking Feedback

a) **Cognitive Biases**: Personal biases can sometimes cloud objective self-assessment (Dunning, Heath, & Suls, 2004).

b) **Fear of Criticism**: Many professionals dread negative feedback, which can hinder the feedback-seeking process (Stone & Heen, 2014).

c) **Misalignment of Feedback**: Feedback, if not aligned with one's role or not actionable, can sometimes be counterproductive (Kluger & DeNisi, 1996).

In the scope of continuous professional development, introspection through self-assessment, complemented by external feedback, emerges as a cornerstone. By understanding their intertwining roles, professionals can craft a more informed, objective, and actionable roadmap for their growth, ensuring that they not only meet but often exceed the benchmarks of excellence in their domain.

Self-Assessment Tools:

As professionals journey through their careers, it becomes indispensable to pause, reflect, and gauge one's progress periodically. One of the most potent mechanisms enabling this introspective analysis is the use of self-assessment tools. These tools, rooted in psychological and pedagogical research, enable individuals to ascertain their strengths, recognize areas of improvement, and consequently, carve a pathway for their professional growth. This chapter unravels the intricate tapestry of self-assessment tools, elucidating their importance, diverse types, methodologies, and their transformative impact on performance and development.

Understanding Self-Assessment

Self-assessment refers to the process where individuals evaluate their own actions, capabilities, and outcomes against predefined standards or criteria (Boud, 1995). It is introspective, often requiring individuals to reflect deeply on their experiences, skills, and aspirations.

Why Self-Assessment is a Cornerstone of Continuous Development

a) **Self-awareness**: It cultivates a profound understanding of one's strengths and weaknesses, pivotal for growth (Drucker, 1999).

b) **Personal Accountability**: Owning one's growth journey fosters a sense of responsibility and proactive development (Zimmerman, 2002).

c) **Tailored Learning Pathways**: Armed with insights from self-assessments, individuals can design personalized development plans (Moon, 2004).

Prominent Self-Assessment Tools

a) **StrengthsFinder**: Developed by the Gallup Organization, this tool helps individuals identify their top strengths, fostering a strengths-based development approach (Rath, 2007).

b) **Myers-Briggs Type Indicator (MBTI)**: A widely-used personality assessment, MBTI offers insights into individual preferences and potential career paths (Myers, 1995).

c) **Emotional Intelligence (EI) Assessments**: Tools such as the Emotional Quotient Inventory (EQ-i) gauge an individual's emotional intelligence, crucial for leadership and interpersonal roles (Bar-On, 2004).

d) **360-Degree Feedback**: This involves gathering feedback from colleagues, subordinates, and supervisors, providing a holistic view of an individual's performance (Edwards & Ewen, 1996).

Implementing Self-Assessment in Professional Development

a) **Integrate in Learning Modules**: Incorporate self-assessment exercises in regular training sessions for immediate feedback (Black & Wiliam, 1998).

b) **Foster a Safe Environment**: Ensure that the organizational culture supports openness, making it easier for employees to engage in honest self-assessment (London, 2003).

c) **Leverage Technology**: Utilize online platforms and apps that offer self-assessment modules and track growth over time (Davies, 2010).

Chapter 6: Performance Through Continuous Development

Challenges in Self-Assessment

a) **Overestimation or Underestimation**: Individuals might either overrate or underrate their capabilities (Dunning, Johnson, Ehrlinger, & Kruger, 2003).

b) **Lack of Objectivity**: Emotional biases can sometimes skew the self-assessment process (Eva & Regehr, 2005).

c) **Feedback Overwhelm**: Without proper guidance, dealing with feedback from tools like 360-degree evaluations can be daunting (Bracken, Timmreck, & Church, 2001).

In the era of rapid professional evolution, being a passive passenger on the journey isn't an option. Self-assessment tools empower individuals to take the wheel, steering their development with insight and intention. They lay the foundation for a culture of introspection, responsibility, and tailored growth, ensuring that professionals are not just reactive but proactive architects of their development trajectory.

Setting personal and professional growth goals:

A pivotal step in the continuous development process is goal-setting. Both at the individual and organizational level, well-defined goals serve as guiding stars, illuminating the path forward, and providing a clear roadmap for progress. This chapter delves into the nuanced process of setting personal and professional growth goals, unraveling their intrinsic value, methodologies, and the transformative impact they have on performance and development.

Understanding the Nature of Growth Goals

Growth goals are aspirational objectives individuals set for themselves, aiming for advancement, learning, and improvement in personal or professional spheres (Locke & Latham, 2006). Distinct from performance goals, which focus on specific outcomes or task accomplishments, growth goals emphasize on the development and mastery of skills or knowledge.

Why Growth Goals Matter

a) **Direction and Focus**: Growth goals offer a clear direction, helping individuals channel their energies and resources effectively (Morisano, Hirsh, Peterson, Pihl, & Shore, 2010).

b) **Motivation**: Well-set goals act as intrinsic motivators, driving individuals to overcome challenges and constantly push their boundaries (Bandura & Schunk, 1981).

c) **Measurement and Feedback**: Goals provide a benchmark against which progress can be measured, allowing for regular feedback and course corrections (Zimmerman, 2008).

Strategies for Effective Goal Setting

a) **SMART Goals**: Ensuring goals are Specific, Measurable, Achievable, Relevant, and Time-bound can significantly enhance their effectiveness (Doran, 1981).

b) **Alignment with Core Values**: Goals that resonate with one's intrinsic values and beliefs are more motivating and fulfilling (Deci & Ryan, 2000).

c) **Seeking Feedback**: Regularly consulting mentors, peers, or supervisors ensures that goals remain relevant and adaptive to changing circumstances (London, 2003).

d) **Periodic Review**: Revisiting and adjusting goals based on achievements, challenges, or changing aspirations is crucial for continuous development (Kaplan & Norton, 2001).

Challenges in Setting Growth Goals

a) **Overambitious Goals**: While ambition is commendable, setting overly challenging goals can lead to burnout and disillusionment (Baumeister, Vohs, & Tice, 2007).

b) **Vague Objectives**: Ambiguous goals can lead to confusion, misdirection, and lack of progress (Locke, Shaw, Saari, & Latham, 1981).

c) **External Pressures**: Sometimes, external pressures from peers, family, or society can skew one's genuine aspirations, leading to misaligned goals (Crocker, Luhtanen, Cooper, & Bouvrette, 2003).

Case Studies: The Transformative Power of Growth Goals

- **Individual Level**: Jane, a mid-level manager, felt stagnated in her role. However, by setting clear growth goals, she charted a path to acquire new skills and transitioned to a more fulfilling leadership role within two years (Herzberg, 1968).

- **Organizational Level**: TechSolutions, a startup, was struggling with high employee turnover. By setting organizational growth goals focusing on employee development, they not only reduced turnover but also improved overall performance (Kaplan & Norton, 1996).

Chapter 6: Performance Through Continuous Development

In the voyage of continuous development, growth goals are the compass. By understanding their significance, adopting strategies for effective goal setting, and navigating associated challenges, professionals can shape a trajectory marked by learning, achievement, and fulfillment.

Encourage the setting of ambitious yet achievable goals:

In the voyage of professional growth and performance enhancement, goal-setting emerges as the compass that offers direction and purpose. Goals serve as the benchmarks against which individuals measure progress, derive motivation, and establish a clear trajectory. However, not all goals are created equal. While ambition can propel individuals towards exceptional achievements, it's paramount that these aspirations remain within the realms of achievability. This chapter embarks on an exploration of striking that balance: setting goals that are both ambitious and achievable, and understanding the transformative power they wield in the sphere of continuous development.

The Philosophy Behind Goal-Setting

Goal-setting is not merely about defining endpoints; it's a strategic process of deciphering where one wants to be, determining the steps to get there, and staying motivated throughout the journey (Locke & Latham, 2002).

The Power of Ambition in Goals

a) **Driving Force**: Ambitious goals act as catalysts, pushing individuals beyond their comfort zones and challenging them to strive for excellence (Collins, 2001).

b) **Innovation**: Higher aspirations often demand innovative solutions, fostering creativity and resourcefulness (Amabile & Khaire, 2008).

The Importance of Achievability

a) **Motivation Maintenance**: Goals that are seen as achievable maintain motivation, while seemingly impossible targets can demotivate and discourage (Bandura & Schunk, 1981).

b) **Tangible Progress**: Achievable goals ensure that individuals experience the satisfaction of progress and accomplishment, crucial for long-term persistence (Deci & Ryan, 2000).

Balancing Ambition with Achievability

a) **SMART Goals**: Goals should be Specific, Measurable, Achievable, Relevant, and Time-bound. This framework ensures that while aspirations are high, they are rooted in reality (Doran, 1981).

b) **Incremental Milestones**: Breaking down a larger goal into smaller, incremental steps can make an ambitious objective feel more achievable (Heath, Larrick, & Wu, 1999).

Real-world Examples of Ambitious Yet Achievable Goals

- **SpaceX**: Elon Musk's vision of colonizing Mars is undeniably ambitious. Yet, through incremental achievements, like the successful landing of rockets, this ambition is presented as achievable (Vance, 2015).

- **Nike's Breaking2 Project**: The project aimed to break the two-hour marathon barrier—a goal seen as both ambitious and borderline unachievable. Through meticulous planning and incremental targets, elite runners came astonishingly close, highlighting the power of setting such goals (Culpepper, 2017).

Challenges in Setting Ambitious Yet Achievable Goals

a) **Overstretching**: There's a fine line between stretching oneself and becoming overwhelmed. Striking this balance can be challenging (Csikszentmihalyi, 1990).

b) **External Pressures**: Sometimes external factors, like industry benchmarks or peer achievements, can pressure individuals into setting goals that may not align with their personal or organizational capacities (Christensen, 1997).

Strategies for Effective Goal Setting

a) **Regular Review**: Periodically reviewing and adjusting goals ensures alignment with changing circumstances and resources (Cervone, Jiwani, & Wood, 1991).

b) **Seek Feedback**: Feedback from peers, mentors, and stakeholders can offer valuable insights into the feasibility and relevance of goals (Hattie & Timperley, 2007).

Conclusion

In the area of continuous development, setting ambitious yet achievable goals is akin to setting one's sails in the direction of favorable winds. While ambition gives the thrust to move forward, achievability ensures that the journey is fulfilling, rewarding, and sustainable. By understanding and implementing the delicate balance between these two facets, professionals and organizations can chart a course to unparalleled growth and success.

Chapter 7: Practical Tips for Immediate Implementation

In the journey towards enhancing staff performance, understanding the theory and principles is only one side of the coin. Equally essential is the ability to translate these theories into actionable steps that can be implemented swiftly and effectively in real-world scenarios. This chapter serves as a bridge between understanding and action. Drawing insights from prior chapters, we present a curated list of practical tips that individuals and organizations can immediately adopt to drive transformation in their professional milieu.

The Rationale for Immediate Implementation

Change, especially in a professional context, often faces inertia. This inertia can stem from a variety of sources: fear of the unknown, complacency, or even just the perceived enormity of the task ahead (Kotter, 1995). Immediate implementation cuts through this inertia. By introducing actionable steps that can be readily adopted, the journey of transformation begins with momentum, setting a positive tone for the ongoing process of enhancement (Lewin, 1947).

In the landscape of organizational change and performance enhancement, the pace at which new strategies and policies are enacted can significantly influence their success. Immediate implementation, as opposed to a protracted rollout, has been gaining traction in modern management philosophies. To truly grasp the potency of this approach, one must understand the underlying rationale. In this section, we delve deeper into the reasons why immediate implementation serves as an effective strategy for boosting staff performance and organizational growth.

The Momentum of Starting Now

The moment a decision for change is made, there's a palpable energy and momentum. Immediate implementation capitalizes on this energy, ensuring that the excitement and commitment do not wane (Kotter, 1996). By harnessing this initial enthusiasm, organizations can drive early success, which in turn acts as a motivator for continued efforts.

Countering Organizational Inertia

Inertia in organizations is the resistance to change, often stemming from comfort with the status quo or fear of the unknown (Hannan & Freeman, 1984). By moving swiftly towards implementation, organizations can outpace this inertia, reducing resistance and facilitating smoother transitions.

Immediate Feedback Loops

Quick implementation allows for faster feedback, ensuring that any necessary adjustments can be made in real-time (Agyris, 1991). This dynamic approach reduces the chances of persisting with ineffective strategies and ensures that resources are allocated efficiently.

Building a Culture of Agility

In today's rapidly changing business environment, agility is a prized attribute. Organizations that can swiftly pivot and adapt have a competitive advantage (Teece, Pisano, & Shuen, 1997). Immediate implementation fosters this agility, making quick decision-making and action a part of the organizational DNA.

Minimizing Uncertainty and Anxiety

Protracted rollouts and implementation processes can lead to prolonged periods of uncertainty, which can breed anxiety among staff (Ashford, Lee, & Bobko, 1989). Immediate action provides clarity and direction, reducing the anxieties associated with ambiguity.

Mitigating External Risks

In the fast-paced world of business, external factors such as market dynamics, competitor actions, and technological advancements can swiftly alter the landscape (Porter, 1980). Immediate implementation reduces the window of vulnerability, ensuring that the organization remains a step ahead.

Immediate implementation isn't just a matter of speed; it's a strategic choice. By understanding its underlying rationale, organizations can make informed decisions, leveraging the power of immediacy to drive meaningful and sustained improvements in staff performance.

Practical Tips for Enhancing Performance

a) **Goal Alignment**: Ensure that individual goals are aligned with team and organizational objectives. This creates coherence and unity in purpose (Locke & Latham, 2006).

b) **Regular Feedback Loops**: Institute a culture of continuous feedback. Weekly or bi-weekly check-ins can provide timely course corrections and recognition (London, 2003).

c) **Invest in Training**: Identify skill gaps and invest in targeted training modules. Consider both formal training and peer-to-peer knowledge sharing sessions (Noe, 2010).

d) **Promote Collaborative Workspaces**: Physical or digital spaces that foster collaboration can enhance team cohesion and idea generation (Allen, 1977).

e) **Encourage Self-assessment**: Make tools and resources available for individuals to periodically evaluate their progress. This fosters personal accountability (Boud, 1995).

Immediate Steps for Workplace Dynamics

a) **Open Door Policy**: Leaders and managers should promote accessibility, encouraging staff to voice concerns, ideas, or seek guidance (Morrison & Milliken, 2000).

b) **Diversity and Inclusion Training**: Foster an environment where all employees feel valued and included. This not only promotes harmony but also drives innovation through diverse perspectives (Cox & Blake, 1991).

c) **Conflict Resolution Mechanisms**: Establish clear protocols to address and resolve conflicts. This ensures that issues are dealt with constructively before they escalate (Rahim, 2002).

Tips for Continuous Development

a) **Personal Development Plans**: Encourage employees to chart out personal development plans, setting clear milestones for their growth journey (Maurer, 2001).

b) **Mentorship Programs**: Pairing seasoned professionals with newer entrants can accelerate learning and foster a culture of knowledge sharing (Ragins & Kram, 2007).

c) **Stay Updated with Industry Trends**: Regularly attend seminars, webinars, or workshops to ensure that the organization and its employees are in sync with industry best practices (Salas, Tannenbaum, Kraiger, & Smith-Jentsch, 2012).

Implementing Change: Challenges & Overcoming Them

Immediate implementation, while advantageous, is not without challenges. Resistance to change, logistical constraints, or even just skepticism can pose hurdles (Oreg, 2003). However, with a clear communication strategy, involvement of all stakeholders in decision-making, and by showcasing early wins, these challenges can be mitigated (Kotter & Schlesinger, 2008).

Embracing the power of immediate implementation offers a plethora of advantages for organizations striving for enhancement. However, this swift action-oriented approach is not without its fair share of challenges. Recognizing and understanding these challenges is the first step to effectively addressing them and ensuring a successful transition.

The Nature of Resistance to Change

One of the foremost challenges organizations face when introducing change is resistance from employees. This resistance can manifest in various forms, from passive non-compliance to active pushback (Dent & Goldberg, 1999). The reasons for this resistance are multifaceted:

a) **Fear of the Unknown**: Employees may be apprehensive about changes because they're unsure how it will affect their roles or the organization at large (Conner, 1992).

b) **Loss of Control**: Significant shifts can leave employees feeling that they've lost control over familiar territories (Strebel, 1996).

c) **Perceived Negative Implications**: Employees might resist if they believe the change will result in unfavorable outcomes, such as increased workload or potential job loss (Coch & French, 1948).

Overcoming Resistance

Successfully navigating these challenges requires a mix of proactive strategies and responsive actions:

a) **Transparent Communication**: By ensuring open channels of communication, organizations can address concerns, clarify misconceptions, and build trust (Lewis, 2006).

b) **Inclusive Decision Making**: Involve employees in the change process. This not only provides them with a sense of ownership but also leverages their insights (Kotter & Schlesinger, 1979).

c) **Provide Training**: Offer training sessions to equip employees with the necessary skills and knowledge, making the transition smoother (Maurer, 1996).

d) **Highlight Early Wins**: By showcasing immediate successes, organizations can build momentum and demonstrate the benefits of the change (Kotter, 1995).

Logistical Challenges

Apart from resistance, organizations might encounter logistical hurdles. Implementing changes swiftly can sometimes strain resources, or highlight system inadequacies.

Overcoming Logistical Challenges

a) **Pilot Programs**: Before a full-scale implementation, testing changes on a smaller scale can identify potential issues (Thomke, 2003).

b) **Resource Allocation**: Ensuring adequate resources – both in terms of manpower and material – can mitigate potential bottlenecks (Galbraith, 1973).

c) **Continuous Review**: Adopt an iterative approach, continuously reviewing and refining the implementation process (Deming, 1986).

Managing External Stakeholder Expectations

Immediate implementation can also impact external stakeholders like customers, suppliers, or investors. Their perceptions and reactions can influence the success of the change (Freeman, 1984).

Strategies for External Stakeholder Management

a) **Stakeholder Communication**: Keep external stakeholders informed about the changes, reasons behind them, and potential benefits (Clarkson, 1995).

b) **Feedback Mechanisms**: Create avenues for stakeholders to voice their concerns or suggestions (Donaldson & Preston, 1995).

Conclusion

While immediate implementation offers a promising approach to organizational enhancement, it's essential to recognize and proactively address the accompanying challenges. With strategic planning, open communication, and a commitment to continuous refinement, organizations can navigate these hurdles and realize the full potential of their change initiatives. While the journey of enhancing staff performance is continuous and evolving, the first steps are crucial. Immediate implementation serves as the impetus, propelling organizations and individuals forward with clarity, purpose, and momentum. By adopting these practical tips, the daunting task ahead becomes a series of manageable, actionable steps, each one bringing us closer to our ultimate vision of excellence.

Dress code dos and don'ts checklist:

Implementing a dress code in an organization is more than just setting guidelines about what to wear. It's about instilling a sense of professionalism, respect, and alignment with organizational values. However, the introduction or modification of dress codes can often be met with resistance or confusion. Providing clear guidelines via a "dos and don'ts" checklist can simplify the process, offering clarity to employees and ensuring smoother transition.

The Relevance of Dress Codes

Historically, dress codes have been emblematic of an organization's culture, values, and the nature of its business (Peluchette & Karl, 2007). For instance, finance and law sectors traditionally lean towards more formal attire, reflecting their formal, high-stakes environments. On the other hand, tech start-ups or creative agencies might embrace a more relaxed dress code, signaling innovation and flexibility.

Dress Code Dos and Don'ts Checklist

Dos:

1. **Clarity**: Clearly outline what constitutes acceptable attire. Use specific examples or visuals if necessary (Rafaeli & Pratt, 1993).

2. **Inclusivity**: Ensure that the dress code does not discriminate against any group. It should respect cultural, religious, and personal choices (Opie, 1998).

3. **Flexibility**: Allow for variations based on roles. A field technician might have different attire needs than a sales executive.

4. **Regular Updates**: Fashion and societal norms evolve. Regularly revisit and update the dress code policies (Postrel, 2003).

5. **Feedback Loop**: Encourage employees to voice their opinions and concerns regarding the dress code, creating a sense of involvement (Miller, 1997).

Don'ts:

1. **Overregulation**: Avoid being too prescriptive. Offering some leeway can help employees feel trusted and respected (Kwon & Parham, 1994).

2. **Ambiguity**: Avoid vague terms like "business casual" without context. This can lead to confusion and inconsistent implementation (Rafaeli & Pratt, 1993).

3. **Ignoring Practicality**: Ensure that the dress code is practical. For instance, mandating heels in an environment that requires a lot of walking can be impractical and even harmful.

4. **Over-enforcement**: While adherence is essential, avoid creating a culture of constant scrutiny and enforcement. It can lead to resentment and reduced morale (Roach-Higgins & Eicher, 1992).

5. **Neglecting Regional Variations**: For organizations spread across different regions or countries, it's essential to factor in local customs, climates, and cultural norms (Crane, 2000).

While a dress code might seem a minor aspect of organizational policy, it can have profound effects on employee morale, organizational image, and even productivity. A thoughtfully crafted and sensitively implemented dress code can seamlessly merge individual expression with organizational values, creating a harmonious work environment.

Effective communication templates:

Effective communication is the backbone of any organizational change, including the introduction of new policies or practices. To ensure that messages are clear, comprehensible, and actionable, it is often beneficial to rely on structured communication templates. These templates serve as frameworks, helping to maintain consistency while allowing for flexibility based on the specific subject matter. Here, we'll explore the importance of these templates, provide some dos and don'ts, and cite relevant literature on the topic.

The Power of Structured Communication

In the vast arena of organizational communication, structured templates provide a roadmap. They ensure that essential points are covered, avoid the pitfalls of ambiguity, and maintain a consistent tone (Argenti, 2007). By utilizing effective communication templates, organizations can foster transparency, build trust, and encourage active engagement among employees (Gillis, 2011).

Communication Template Dos and Don'ts Checklist

Dos:

1. **Clarity**: Ensure that every message is clear, precise, and free from jargon. A well-understood message is more likely to be acted upon (Cornelissen, 2014).

2. **Relevance**: Tailor the communication to its target audience, ensuring it's relevant and resonates with them (Bordia et al., 2004).

3. **Consistency**: Even though the content might change, maintaining a consistent format helps in familiarizing the audience with organizational communication (Fairhurst & Sarr, 1996).

4. **Feedback Channels**: Always include avenues for feedback, enabling a two-way communication process (Grunig, 1992).

5. **Regular Updates**: In situations of ongoing change, periodic updates can help alleviate uncertainties and manage expectations (DiFonzo & Bordia, 1998).

Don'ts:

1. **Information Overload**: Avoid overwhelming employees with too much information. It's better to be concise and direct (Eppler & Mengis, 2004).

2. **Assuming Prior Knowledge**: Do not assume that everyone is on the same page. Recapitulate essential points if necessary (Gudykunst, 2004).

3. **Neglecting Emotional Aspects**: Especially in significant changes, acknowledge the emotional dimension. Recognize concerns and offer reassurance (Heath, 1997).

4. **Ignoring Feedback**: Never neglect the feedback received. Addressing concerns or suggestions can foster a more inclusive environment (Ilgen, Fisher, & Taylor, 1979).

5. **Inconsistent Mediums**: While it's important to utilize various communication channels, ensure the message remains consistent across all mediums (Shirky, 2008).

In the era of information overload, well-structured and effective communication has never been more critical. By adhering to the above dos and don'ts and leveraging structured templates, organizations can ensure that their messages are not only heard but also understood, accepted, and acted upon.

Conflict resolution role-playing scenarios:

Role-playing has emerged as a crucial tool in the domain of organizational training and development, especially when it pertains to conflict resolution (Alden, 1981). By placing participants in scenarios that mimic real-world challenges, they're given an opportunity to practice their responses, garner feedback, and refine their approach in a controlled setting. This immersive experience equips individuals with the confidence and skill to navigate conflicts when they occur in real-time.

Understanding the Dynamics of Conflict

Before delving into the scenarios, it's essential to grasp the nature of workplace conflict. Conflicts can arise from various sources, including differing values, competition for resources, communication breakdowns, or unmet expectations (De Dreu, 2008). Resolving these conflicts effectively requires a mix of empathy, communication, and problem-solving skills (Fisher & Ury, 1981).

Conflict Resolution Role-Playing Scenarios Checklist

Dos:

1. **Diversity in Scenarios**: Ensure the role-playing exercises encompass a range of conflicts – from inter-personal disagreements to departmental resource allocation challenges (Tjosvold, 1991).

2. **Safe Environment**: Create an atmosphere where participants feel safe to express their thoughts, make mistakes, and learn (Kolb, 1984).

3. **Immediate Feedback**: After each role-playing session, offer constructive feedback, highlighting areas of strength and suggesting improvements (Hunton & Gold, 2010).

4. **Encourage Reflection**: Urge participants to reflect on their performance, identify their emotional triggers, and consider alternative strategies (Schön, 1987).

5. **Realism**: Ensure that the scenarios are as close to real-life situations as possible, making the learning experience more relevant (Joyce & Showers, 2002).

Don'ts:

1. **Overwhelming Complexity**: While realism is essential, avoid creating scenarios so complex that participants lose sight of the core conflict and its resolution (Gordon, 1977).

2. **Biased Feedback**: Avoid feedback that favors a particular style of conflict resolution; instead, promote adaptability (Rahim, 1983).

3. **Neglecting Follow-up**: Merely conducting role-playing sessions isn't enough. Periodic refresher sessions can reinforce learning (Knowles, 1980).

4. **Disregarding Emotional Aspects**: Conflicts can be emotionally charged. Ignoring the emotional dimension can render the role-playing exercise ineffective (Jordan & Troth, 2004).

5. **Rigid Scripting**: While a structure is essential, allow participants some leeway to think on their feet, mirroring real-world unpredictability (Argyris, 1980).

Conflict resolution role-playing can be a transformative tool for organizations, fostering a harmonious workplace. However, its success hinges on the thoughtful design of scenarios, a supportive environment, and an emphasis on continuous learning.

Feedback and evaluation forms:

Feedback and evaluation are intrinsic parts of the organizational learning process. They provide valuable insights into performance, behaviors, and outcomes. When collected systematically through well-designed forms, this feedback can lead to actionable intelligence that catalyzes both personal and organizational growth. By understanding the design and utility of feedback and evaluation forms, organizations can harness their potential to create a more efficient, effective, and engaged workforce.

Importance of Structured Feedback

Feedback, when delivered constructively and systematically, can be transformative. Research by London (1995) suggests that feedback can lead to enhanced self-awareness, clarity on job expectations, and improved performance. Evaluation forms, as structured mediums for feedback collection, ensure the process is organized, comprehensive, and can be analyzed to draw meaningful insights (Smither, 1998).

Key Considerations for Feedback and Evaluation Forms

Dos:

1. **Clarity**: The questions or prompts should be clear and precise, minimizing any room for ambiguity (Roberts, 2003).

2. **Relevance**: Ensure every element on the form directly correlates with the objectives of the feedback process (DeNisi & Kluger, 2000).

3. **Anonymity**: In many situations, anonymous feedback can lead to more candid and objective responses (Ilgen, Fisher, & Taylor, 1979).

4. **Scalability**: Use scales (e.g., Likert scales) for quantifiable feedback that allows for easy analysis and comparison (Spector, 1994).

5. **Open-ended Sections**: Include spaces for qualitative feedback, giving respondents the chance to provide insights not covered by structured questions (Brett & Atwater, 2001).

Don'ts:

1. **Overwhelming Length**: Avoid excessively long forms. They can be tedious, leading to rushed responses or even incompletion (Riggio, 2003).

2. **Loaded Questions**: Stay away from leading or biased questions which can skew results (Dipboye & de Pontbriand, 1981).

3. **Complex Language**: Avoid jargon or complex language. Forms should be comprehensible to everyone in the target audience (Harrison, 1995).

4. **Neglecting Follow-up**: Just collecting feedback isn't enough. Ensure there's a system in place to act on the insights (Ashford, 1986).

5. **Static Design**: The design shouldn't be static. Periodically review and update the form based on evolving needs (Mount, 1983).

Feedback and evaluation forms are powerful tools. When designed thoughtfully, they not only gather data but can also shape behaviors, align expectations, and foster a culture of continuous improvement. By following best practices, organizations can use these tools to drive meaningful, positive change.

Actionable Steps that can immediately implemented:

One of the major challenges organizations often face after training or development interventions is translating the learned concepts into immediate action. To ensure that knowledge transition happens seamlessly and effectively, it's essential to provide readers or participants with actionable steps that are both straightforward and applicable in real-world settings. These steps act as a bridge between theory and practice, enabling individuals to make tangible progress and witness immediate improvements (Knowles, 1980).

The Need for Actionable Steps

According to Bandura's Social Learning Theory (1977), individuals learn best when they are given the opportunity to practice what they've learned in a safe environment and receive feedback on their actions. By providing actionable steps, we cater to this need for 'doing' as a form of reinforcement and learning.

Actionable Steps for Immediate Implementation

1. **Setting Clear Objectives**: Before starting any task or project, clearly define what you intend to achieve. This step ensures focus and provides a metric for success (Locke & Latham, 1990).

2. **Time Management**: Allocate specific time slots in your daily or weekly schedule to work on new initiatives or changes. Tools like the Eisenhower Box can help prioritize tasks based on their urgency and importance (Covey, 1989).

3. **Seek Feedback**: Regularly consult with peers or supervisors about the changes you're implementing. Feedback serves as a corrective mechanism, ensuring that you're on the right track (Ilgen, Fisher, & Taylor, 1979).

4. **Maintain a Reflection Journal**: Documenting your experiences, challenges, and learnings can provide valuable insights into your progress and areas of improvement (Schön, 1983).

5. **Small Group Collaborations**: Form or join small teams within the organization that share a common goal. Collective effort often leads to better solutions and mutual motivation (Wenger, 1998).

6. **Continuous Learning**: Dedicate some time each week for upskilling. This can be through online courses, workshops, or reading. Keeping the learning momentum ensures adaptability in dynamic environments (Argyris, 1991).

7. **Celebrate Small Wins**: Recognize and celebrate small achievements. This not only boosts morale but also reinforces the belief that change is beneficial and achievable (Amabile & Kramer, 2011).

Actionable steps are the cornerstone of practical application. They transform abstract ideas into concrete actions, driving real change and improvement. By adhering to these steps, individuals and organizations can ensure that their learning is not just confined to books or training rooms but is actively reflected in their daily operations and behaviors.

Share quick tips, tricks, and techniques:

Quick implementation tools are the backbone of efficient change management. These tangible takeaways serve as the catalysts that propel individuals and organizations from understanding to action, transforming theory into daily practice. They are especially valuable in today's fast-paced work environment, where adaptability and speed are at a premium (Fullan, 2001).

Rationale Behind Quick Implementation Tools

As Duhigg (2012) outlines in his exploration of habit formation, small, immediate changes can trigger a ripple effect, leading to broader organizational transformation. Quick tips and tricks provide an accessible entry point, reducing the inertia of change and catalyzing broader progress.

Quick Tips, Tricks, and Techniques for Immediate Implementation

1. **The Two-minute Rule**: If something takes less than two minutes, do it immediately. This rule, derived from David Allen's *Getting Things Done* methodology, is a powerful tool against procrastination (Allen, 2001).

2. **The Pomodoro Technique**: Utilize focused work sessions (typically 25 minutes long) followed by short breaks. This cycle boosts productivity and maintains high levels of focus (Cirillo, 2006).

3. **SMART Goal Setting**: When setting goals, ensure they are Specific, Measurable, Achievable, Relevant, and Time-bound (Doran, 1981).

4. **Feedback Sandwich**: When providing feedback, start with a positive note, follow with constructive criticism, and then conclude with another positive statement. This structure facilitates a more receptive environment for feedback (Silverman, Kurtz, & Draper, 1996).

5. **The 5-Whys Technique**: When faced with a problem, ask "why" five times to get to the root cause. This simple iterative

technique, originated from Toyota's production system, is essential for effective problem-solving (Ohno, 1988).

6. **Batching Tasks**: Group similar tasks together and tackle them in dedicated time slots. This technique minimizes the mental load of switching between different types of tasks and enhances efficiency (Rogers & Monsell, 1995).

7. **Visual Management Tools**: Utilize visual aids like Kanban boards or Gantt charts to track progress, manage workflows, and identify bottlenecks (Hines & Rich, 1997).

8. **Stay Updated with Microlearning**: Adopt bite-sized learning sessions, often 5-10 minutes long, focusing on a single concept. This approach is effective for rapidly updating skills and knowledge (Hug, 2005).

In the vast landscape of organizational development, sometimes the simplest techniques yield the most profound results. By embracing these quick tips, tricks, and techniques, organizations can foster an environment of continuous improvement, driving both personal and collective growth.

Templates and scenarios for real-life situations:

Templates and scenario-based learning have been recognized as valuable assets in training and development literature. They not only bridge the gap between theory and practice but also offer a structured approach to real-life challenges, enabling individuals and organizations to navigate complexities with confidence (Kindley, 2002).

The Power of Templates and Scenarios

Chapter 7: Practical Tips for Immediate Implementation

Scenarios present hypothetical, yet realistic, situations that challenge the learner to think critically, make decisions, and witness the outcomes of those decisions (Schank, Berman, & Macpherson, 1999). Templates, on the other hand, provide a structured framework, guiding individuals through processes or procedures. Together, they form a powerful duo in organizational training, ensuring practicality and effectiveness (Rogers, 2001).

Templates and Scenarios for Real-life Situations

1. **Conflict Resolution Template**:

   - Description of the conflict

   - Parties involved

   - Initial responses and reactions

   - Recommended resolution steps

   - Feedback and outcome

Scenario: A team member consistently misses deadlines, causing delays in project delivery. The team is frustrated. How should the project manager approach this?

2. **Performance Feedback Template**:

   - Employee's name and position

   - Period of review

   - Achievements and strengths

   - Areas for improvement

- Actionable recommendations

Scenario: A sales associate has exceeded her quarterly targets but struggles with teamwork and often works in isolation. How should the supervisor provide feedback?

3. **Project Planning Template**:

- Project name and description

- Objective(s)

- Key stakeholders

- Milestones and deadlines

- Risks and mitigation strategies

Scenario: The marketing department is launching a new product. What steps should they follow to ensure a successful launch?

4. **Team Building Activity Scenario**:

- Objective of the activity

- Description of the activity

- Required materials

- Steps for execution

- Feedback and reflection session

Scenario: A team is facing communication breakdowns. The team leader wants to conduct an activity to foster open communication and trust.

5. **Crisis Management Template**:

- Nature of the crisis

- Immediate response actions

- Communication plan (internal and external)

- Long-term recovery and mitigation strategies

Scenario: A cybersecurity breach has compromised client data. How should the IT department respond?

Templates and scenarios empower individuals to approach challenges methodically and thoughtfully. By offering structured guidance and hypothetical situations for practice, they ensure that employees are equipped to manage real-world challenges with confidence and expertise.

The continuous journey of personal and professional growth:

The pursuit of personal and professional growth is a lifelong endeavor, representing an individual's commitment to bettering themselves and enhancing their skills and abilities over time. This journey often intertwines personal ambitions with professional aspirations, influencing decision-making processes, career trajectories, and even interpersonal relationships.

Understanding the Interconnectedness of Personal and Professional Growth

Personal and professional growth, though distinct in their own right, are deeply intertwined. One's personal development—like building resilience, empathy, and critical thinking—can significantly bolster their professional capabilities. Conversely, professional growth, such as acquiring a new skill set, can influence personal identities and shape life's meaning and purpose (Kegan, 1982).

Benefits of Continuous Growth

1. **Adaptability**: In an ever-evolving world, continuous growth ensures individuals remain relevant and adaptable to changes in their professional industries (Bridges, 2009).

2. **Enhanced Satisfaction**: Personal and professional development often leads to increased job satisfaction, as individuals feel more competent and valued in their roles (Judge et al., 1993).

3. **Resilience**: Continuous growth equips individuals with the tools to handle setbacks more effectively, building resilience (Masten, 2001).

4. **Broadened Horizons**: As individuals grow, they often expand their networks, opening doors to new opportunities and experiences (Granovetter, 1973).

The Role of Reflection in Growth

Reflection is a cornerstone of personal and professional growth. By actively reflecting on experiences, successes, and failures, individuals can gain deeper insights into their actions and decisions, leading to more informed choices in the future (Schön, 1983).

Challenges to Continuous Growth

While the journey of continuous growth is rewarding, it is not without its challenges:

a) **Complacency**: Falling into a comfort zone can hinder the pursuit of new learning opportunities (Argyris, 1991).

b) **Lack of Direction**: Without clear goals or objectives, one may struggle to find a path for their growth (Locke & Latham, 2002).

c) **External Barriers**: External factors, such as limited access to resources or opportunities, can impede growth (Bandura, 1977).

Strategies for Ensuring Continuous Growth

a) **Lifelong Learning**: Embrace a mindset of constant learning, seeking knowledge both formally and informally (Jarvis, 2009).

b) **Mentorship**: Engage in mentor-mentee relationships for guidance, knowledge sharing, and perspective (Kram, 1985).

c) **Goal Setting**: Regularly set and reassess personal and professional goals to maintain direction and motivation (Locke & Latham, 2006).

The continuous journey of personal and professional growth is a testament to an individual's dedication to self-improvement. With reflection, resilience, and a commitment to lifelong learning, individuals can navigate the complexities of this journey, reaping its many rewards.

Encouraging a culture of learning and development:

In a world characterized by rapid technological advancements, shifting market dynamics, and evolving workforce expectations, fostering a culture of continuous learning and development (L&D) has become paramount for organizations. This is not merely to stay competitive but to thrive and pave the way for future innovations.

Understanding the Importance of a Learning Culture

A learning culture is one where employees are motivated to continuously expand their skills and knowledge. This isn't just about formal training but encompasses all avenues of learning, including on-the-job experiences, mentorship, and self-directed learning. Senge (1990) described organizations with a robust learning culture as "learning organizations" — entities where new and expansive patterns of thinking are nurtured, collective aspiration is set free, and where individuals continually learn how to learn together.

Benefits of a Learning and Development Culture

a) **Adaptability**: A culture of L&D prepares organizations to quickly adapt to changes, whether it's market shifts, technological advancements, or global events (Garvin, 1993).

b) **Enhanced Employee Engagement**: Employees in a learning environment feel more valued and challenged, leading to increased motivation and retention (Noe, 2010).

c) **Innovation Boost**: Continuous learning often sparks innovation as employees are exposed to new ideas and techniques (Nonaka & Takeuchi, 1995).

Promoting a Culture of Learning and Development

a) **Leadership Endorsement**: Leaders play a pivotal role in fostering a culture of learning. By being advocates and participants of continuous learning, leaders can set the tone for the entire organization (Yukl, 2012).

b) **Collaborative Learning**: Encouraging team-based learning, knowledge sharing sessions, and cross-functional projects can facilitate collaborative learning experiences (Brown & Duguid, 1991).

c) **Personalized Learning Pathways**: Recognizing that one size does not fit all, personalized learning experiences cater to individual needs, learning styles, and career aspirations (Clark & Mayer, 2016).

d) **Leveraging Technology**: Modern Learning Management Systems (LMS) and online platforms can deliver a diverse range of training materials, from e-courses to webinars, catering to different learning preferences (Allen & Seaman, 2017).

Challenges in Fostering a Learning Culture

a) **Resistance to Change**: Some employees might resist the shift towards continuous learning, especially if they feel it diverts from their core tasks or pressures them into "classroom" settings (Oreg, 2003).

b) **Budget Constraints**: High-quality training programs, tools, and systems require financial investments, and budget restrictions can be a limiting factor (Parry & Thompson, 2007).

Measuring the Impact

It's essential to measure the impact of L&D initiatives to ensure they're yielding desired outcomes and to refine strategies as needed. This can be done through performance metrics, feedback surveys, and more sophisticated methods like return on investment (ROI) analyses for training programs (Phillips, 1996).

Appendices

Sample dress code policies:

In today's dynamic business environment, the way employees present themselves plays a significant role in an organization's branding, public image, and internal culture. Dress code policies, often considered a nuanced aspect of human resources management, hold the potential to influence the workplace in ways that may go beyond just aesthetics. With an array of corporate cultures ranging from the traditional to the more avant-garde, dress codes have evolved to reflect these shifts (Peluchette & Karl, 2007).

Understanding the Evolution of Dress Codes

Historically, workplaces, especially in sectors like finance, law, and consulting, had stringent formal dress codes. Over time, especially with the emergence of sectors like technology and creative industries, a more relaxed, 'business casual' or even 'casual' dress code became prevalent (Gotsi, Andriopoulos, Lewis, & Ingram, 2010). The intent of a dress code has always been multi-faceted: to ensure employees are safe, to maintain a certain organizational image, and to cultivate a conducive working environment (Rafaeli, Dutton, Harquail, & Mackie-Lewis, 1997).

Dress Codes and Organizational Image

The dress code of an organization's workforce often serves as a direct reflection of its brand image. Employees, when interacting with customers, clients, or other stakeholders, become the face of the company. Their attire, thus, communicates a message about the company's values, professionalism, and culture. For instance, customer-facing roles in high-end industries might require more formal attire to convey a sense of professionalism and luxury (Kwon & Parham, 1994).

Employee Morale, Productivity, and Dress Codes

While it's evident that dress codes impact external perceptions, they also influence internal dynamics. Research suggests that what employees wear can affect their self-perception, confidence, and even productivity. Some studies indicate that more formal attire might lead to higher abstract thinking and more authoritative behaviors, proving the old adage of 'dressing for success' (Adam & Galinsky, 2012). However, allowing flexibility and autonomy in dress can also boost morale, as it might make employees feel more comfortable and authentic at work (Michael, W., 2006).

Balancing Flexibility and Professionalism

The challenge for many organizations lies in drafting a dress code policy that balances the need for professionalism with the desire for individual expression and comfort. Too stringent a policy might stifle creativity and lead to dissatisfaction, while an overly relaxed code might not convey the desired level of professionalism (Hughes, 2002).

Inclusion and Diversity in Dress Codes

Modern dress code policies also need to consider cultural, religious, and personal choices. Policies should be inclusive, accommodating attire essential for religious beliefs or cultural practices, for instance (Syed & Özbilgin, 2009). Similarly, with a growing recognition of gender fluidity, dress codes should avoid reinforcing binary gender norms.

The Appendices

The forthcoming appendices will present sample dress code policies catering to a range of corporate cultures – from the strictly formal to the relaxed. These samples will serve as a guide for organizations looking to either draft a new policy or amend an existing one. They will reflect contemporary understanding, emphasizing flexibility, inclusivity, and diversity while ensuring the organizational brand and ethos are consistently represented.

Team building activity ideas:

In the ever-evolving business landscape, the need for cohesive, well-integrated teams has never been more paramount. A team that communicates effectively, collaborates seamlessly, and trusts one another can be the difference between project success and failure. Beyond these immediate benefits, team-building activities can influence the overall culture of an organization, fostering an environment where individuals feel valued, understood, and aligned with their peers and the broader company vision (Klein, DiazGranados, Salas, Le, Burke, Lyons, & Goodwin, 2009).

The Evolution of Team Building

Historically, team building was often limited to corporate retreats and occasional office games. Over the years, however, there has been a growing recognition of the multifaceted benefits of team-building exercises. These activities have evolved to include not only physical challenges but also cognitive exercises, creative tasks, and even digital activities suited for remote teams (Widmeyer & Ducharme, 1997). With the rise of global teams and remote working, especially in light of the

Appendices

COVID-19 pandemic, the methods and mediums for team building have transformed significantly (Kniffin et al., 2021).

The Multifaceted Importance of Team Building

A. Enhancing Communication: The foundation of any effective team lies in its ability to communicate. Activities that necessitate dialogue and understanding can break down silos and foster open channels of communication (Dyer, Dyer, & Dyer, 2007).

B. Boosting Morale: Team-building activities often provide a break from routine, allowing employees to engage in a relaxed environment. This can be crucial for morale, providing rejuvenation and a renewed sense of purpose (Tannenbaum, Beard, & Salas, 1992).

C. Uncovering Hidden Talents: Through varied exercises, employees often get to showcase skills and talents that aren't always visible in their day-to-day roles. This can help management in recognizing potential and aiding in succession planning (Guzzo & Dickson, 1996).

D. Building Trust: Trust is a cornerstone of effective teams. Activities that require reliance on one another can help build this vital component of teamwork (DeChurch & Mesmer-Magnus, 2010).

E. Encouraging Collaboration: Modern work often requires cross-functional collaboration. Team-building exercises can help break departmental barriers and encourage a more collaborative work culture (Mathieu, Maynard, Rapp, & Gilson, 2008).

Trends in Team Building

With technology becoming an integral part of work, many team-building exercises have shifted online, catering to the rise in remote and hybrid working models. Virtual escape rooms, online quizzes, and collaborative digital projects have become popular. However, the traditional in-person activities, ranging from outdoor adventures to indoor workshops, remain relevant and beneficial (Bhagat, Kedia, Harveston, & Triandis, 2002).

In the Appendices

The subsequent appendices will present a curated list of team-building activities, segregated based on their modality (physical, cognitive, creative, digital), the size of the team they cater to, and their objectives (communication enhancement, trust-building, etc.). These will serve as a comprehensive resource for organizations, HR professionals, and team leads to select activities best suited to their team's unique needs and contexts.

Customer service training resources:

The business adage, "The customer is always right," has steered the commercial world for decades. Yet, in today's highly competitive, rapidly evolving marketplace, simply accepting this notion isn't enough. Enterprises must deeply embed a culture of exceptional customer service. But how can they ensure that each employee—whether they are on the frontline or behind the scenes—reflects the values, standards, and expertise needed? The answer lies in effective, ongoing customer service training.

Customer service can be the make-or-break factor for a business. According to the American Express Service Barometer, more than two-thirds of American customers are willing to spend more with companies known for outstanding service (American Express, 2017).

Appendices

Given this, it's clear why comprehensive training resources are a business imperative.

Unraveling the Fabric of Exceptional Customer Service

The scope of customer service is vast and complex. It isn't just about handling queries or resolving complaints. Exceptional service weaves together a tapestry of elements, including understanding customer needs, showcasing product knowledge, demonstrating empathy, and managing complex situations and emotions—all while maintaining professionalism and brand consistency (Parasuraman, Zeithaml, & Berry, 1988).

Why Training is Paramount

a) **Evolving Customer Expectations:** With digitalization, global marketplaces, and instant feedback loops, customer expectations are continuously evolving. Training ensures that staff are updated on current industry standards and customer preferences (Maklan, Klaus, & Peacock, 2015).

b) **Maintaining Brand Image:** Employees are the face of the company. Through consistent training, businesses can ensure that their brand image remains untarnished, regardless of whom the customer interacts with (Lacey & Suh, 2010).

c) **Employee Empowerment:** A well-trained employee feels more confident and empowered to handle diverse situations, ultimately leading to higher job satisfaction and reduced turnover (Heskett, Jones, Loveman, Sasser, & Schlesinger, 2008).

The Umbrella of Training Resources

Training resources, especially in the domain of customer service, are diverse. They can range from formal classroom sessions to on-the-job training, from digital modules to role-playing scenarios. The emergence of technologies like Virtual Reality (VR) and Augmented Reality (AR) has further revolutionized how training can be delivered, offering immersive, real-world simulations in a controlled environment (Chung, Lee, & Rao, 2016).

In the Appendices

This section will provide an extensive compilation of customer service training resources. This collection will cater to a broad spectrum of requirements—from foundational principles for new employees to advanced modules for seasoned professionals. These resources will encompass different training methods, platforms, and technologies, ensuring relevance for diverse business models and scales.

References

- Aaker, D. A., Kumar, V., Day, G. S., & Lawley, M. (2004). *Marketing research*. John Wiley & Sons, Inc.

- Accenture (2018). *Pulse check 2018: Taking the pulse of the hyper-relevant consumer*. Accenture Interactive.

- Accenture (2018). *Pulse check 2018: Taking the pulse of the hyper-relevant consumer*. Accenture Interactive.

- Adam, H., & Galinsky, A. D. (2012). Enclothed cognition. *Journal of Experimental Social Psychology, 48*(4), 918-925.

- Aguinis, H., & Kraiger, K. (2009). Benefits of training and development for individuals and teams, organizations, and society. *Annual Review of Psychology, 60*, 451-474.

- Agyris, C. (1991). Teaching smart people how to learn. *Harvard Business Review, 69*(3), 99-109.

- Alden, D. (1981). Role-playing in organizational training. *Training & Development Journal, 35*(2), 70-72.

- Allen, D. (2001). *Getting things done: The art of stress-free productivity*. Penguin.

- Allen, I. E., & Seaman, J. (2017). *Digital learning compass: Distance education enrollment report 2017*. Babson Survey Research Group.

- Allen, T. D., Eby, L. T., O'Brien, K. E., & Lentz, E. (2008). The state of mentoring research: A qualitative review of current research methods and future research implications. *Journal of Vocational Behavior, 73*(3), 343-357.

- Allen, T. D., Golden, T. D., & Shockley, K. M. (2015). How effective is telecommuting? Assessing the status of our scientific findings. *Psychological Science in the Public Interest, 16*(2), 40-68.

- Allen, T. J. (1977). *Managing the flow of technology: Technology transfer and the dissemination of technological information within the R&D organization*. MIT Press.

- Altman, I. (1975). *The environment and social behavior: Privacy, personal space, territory, and crowding*. Brooks/Cole Publishing Company.

- Altschuld, J. W., & Kumar, D. D. (2010). *Needs assessment*. Sage.

- Amabile, T., & Kramer, S. J. (2011). *The progress principle: Using small wins to ignite joy, engagement, and creativity at work*. Harvard Business Press.

- Ambady, N., & Rosenthal, R. (1992). Thin slices of expressive behavior as predictors of interpersonal consequences: A meta-analysis. *Psychological Bulletin, 111*(2), 256-274.

- Ambrosini, V., & Bowman, C. (2009). What are dynamic capabilities and are they a useful construct in strategic

References

- management? *International Journal of Management Reviews, 11*(1), 29-49.

- American Express. (2017). *2017 American Express Customer Service Barometer.* Retrieved from American Express website.

- Anderson, E. W., & Mittal, V. (2000). Strengthening the satisfaction-profit chain. *Journal of Service Research, 3*(2), 107-120.

- Anseel, F., Lievens, F., & Schollaert, E. (2009). Reflection as a strategy to enhance task performance after feedback. *Organizational Behavior and Human Decision Processes, 110*(1), 23-35.

- Argenti, P. A. (2007). *Corporate communication.* Boston: McGraw-Hill/Irwin.

- Argyris, C. (1977). Organizational learning and management information systems. *Accounting, Organizations and Society, 2*(2), 113-123.

- Argyris, C. (1980). Some limitations of the case method: Experiences in a management development program. *Academy of Management Review, 5*(2), 291-298.

- Argyris, C. (1991). *Teaching smart people how to learn.* Harvard Business Review, 4-15.

- Argyris, C., & Schön, D. A. (1974). *Theory in practice: Increasing professional effectiveness.* Jossey-Bass.

- Armstrong, M., & Overton, T. S. (2007). Estimating nonresponse bias in mail surveys. *Journal of Marketing Research, 14*(3), 396-402.

- Arthur, M. B., Khapova, S. N., & Wilderom, C. P. (2005). Career success in a boundaryless career world. *Journal of Organizational Behavior, 26*(2), 177-202.

- Ashford, S. J. (1986). Feedback-seeking in individual adaptation: A resource perspective.

- Ashford, S. J. (1986). Feedback-seeking in individual adaptation: A resource perspective. *Academy of Management Journal, 29*(3), 465-487.

- Ashford, S. J., & Cummings, L. L. (1983). Feedback as an individual resource: Personal strategies of creating information. *Organizational Behavior and Human Performance, 32*(3), 370-398.

- Ashford, S. J., Blatt, R., & VandeWalle, D. (2003). Reflections on the looking glass: A review of research on feedback-seeking behavior in organizations. *Journal of Management, 29*(6), 773-799.

- Ashford, S. J., Lee, C., & Bobko, P. (1989). Content, cause, and consequences of job insecurity: A theory-based measure and substantive test. *Academy of Management Journal, 32*(4), 803-829.

References

- Ashforth, B. E., Kreiner, G. E., & Fugate, M. (2000). All in a day's work: Boundaries and micro role transitions. *Academy of Management Review, 25*(3), 472-491.

- Aspin, D. N., & Chapman, J. D. (2000). Lifelong learning: Concepts and conceptions. *International Journal of Lifelong Education, 19*(1), 2-19.

- Augsburger, D. W. (1992). *Conflict mediation across cultures: Pathways and patterns.* Westminster John Knox Press.

- Avey, J. B., Luthans, F., & Jensen, S. M. (2010). Psychological capital: A positive resource for combating employee stress and turnover. *Human Resource Management, 48*(5), 677-693.

- Aydin, S., & Özer, G. (2005). The analysis of antecedents of customer loyalty in the Turkish mobile telecommunication market. *European Journal of Marketing, 39*(7/8), 910-925.

- Bailey, D. E., & Kurland, N. B. (2002). A review of telework research: Findings, new directions, and lessons for the study of modern work. *Journal of Organizational Behavior, 23*(4), 383-400.

- Bain & Company. (2016). *Customer experience tools and trends.* Bain & Company, Inc.

- Balcazar, F. E., Hopkins, B. L., & Suarez, Y. (1985). A critical, objective review of performance feedback. *Journal of Organizational Behavior Management, 7*(3-4), 65-89.

- Bamberger, P. A., Meshoulam, I., & Biron, M. (2014). *Human resource strategy: Formulation, implementation, and impact.* Routledge.

- Bandura, A. (1977). Self-efficacy: Toward a unifying theory of behavioral change. *Psychological Review, 84*(2), 191.

- Bandura, A. (1977). *Social learning theory.* Prentice Hall.

- Bandura, A., & Schunk, D. H. (1981). Cultivating competence, self-efficacy, and intrinsic interest through proximal self-motivation. *Journal of Personality and Social Psychology, 41*(3), 586-598.

- Barker, R. G. (2007). On-line mentoring for health care leadership development. *Journal of Healthcare Management, 52*(5), 319-329.

- Bar-On, R. (2004). The Bar-On Emotional Quotient Inventory (EQ-i): Rationale, description, and summary of psychometric properties. In G. Geher (Ed.), *Measuring emotional intelligence: Common ground and controversy* (pp. 115-145). Nova Science Publishers.

- Barrick, M. R., & Mount, M. K. (1991). The big five personality dimensions and job performance: A meta-analysis. *Personnel Psychology, 44*(1), 1-26.

- Bartel, A. P. (1994). Productivity gains from the implementation of employee training programs. *Industrial Relations: A Journal of Economy and Society, 33*(4), 411-425.

References

- Bartel, A. P. (1994). Productivity gains from the implementation of employee training programs. *Industrial Relations: A Journal of Economy and Society, 33*(4), 411-425.

- Bass, B. M. (1985). *Leadership and performance beyond expectations*. Free Press.

- Bass, B. M. (1999). *Two decades of research and development in transformational leadership*. European Journal of Work and Organizational Psychology, 8(1), 9-32.

- Bass, B. M. (1999). *Two decades of research and development in transformational leadership*. European Journal of Work and Organizational Psychology, 8(1), 9-32.

- Belbin, R. M. (1981). *Management teams: Why they succeed or fail*. Butterworth-Heinemann.

- Belk, R. W. (1988). Possessions and the extended self. *Journal of Consumer Research, 15*(2), 139-168.

- Belkic, K. L., Landsbergis, P. A., Schnall, P. L., & Baker, D. (2004). Is job strain a major source of cardiovascular disease risk? *Scandinavian Journal of Work, Environment & Health, 30*(2), 85-128.

- Benson, G. S., & Brown, M. (2007). Knowledge worker motivation: The role of the work environment. *Human Resource Development International, 10*(4), 385-400.

- Bercovitch, J., & Jackson, R. (2009). *Conflict resolution in the twenty-first century: Principles, methods, and approaches*. University of Michigan Press.

- Berry, L. L. (1999). Discovering the soul of service. *Free Press*.

- Bhagat, R. S., Kedia, B. L., Harveston, P. D., & Triandis, H. C. (2002). Cultural variations in the cross-border transfer of organizational knowledge: An integrative framework. *Academy of Management Review, 27*(2), 204-221.

- Billett, S. (2001). Learning in the workplace: Strategies for effective practice. Allen & Unwin.

- Billett, S. (2010). Lifelong learning and the workplace: Issues and challenges for workplace practice. *Relating practice and research in adult education and learning*, 147-158.

- Birdwhistell, R. L. (1970). *Kinesics and context: Essays on body motion communication*. University of Pennsylvania Press.

- Bishop, G. D. (1997). Examining possible antecedents of the experience of feeling understood in the conflict arena. *Human Communication Research, 24*(1), 87-114.

- Bitner, M. J. (1990). Evaluating service encounters: the effects of physical surroundings and employee responses. *Journal of Marketing, 54*(2), 69-82.

- Bitner, M. J., Booms, B. H., & Tetreault, M. S. (1990). The service encounter: diagnosing favorable and unfavorable incidents. *Journal of Marketing, 54*(1), 71-84.

- Bitner, M. J., Brown, S. W., & Meuter, M. L. (1997). Technology infusion in service encounters. *Journal of the Academy of Marketing Science, 25*(1), 50-61.

References

- Black, P., & Wiliam, D. (1998). Assessment and classroom learning. *Assessment in Education: Principles, Policy & Practice, 5*(1), 7-74.

- Bleier, A., & Eisenbeiss, M. (2015). Personalized online advertising effectiveness: The interplay of what, when, and where. *Marketing Science, 34*(5), 669-688.

- Blumer, H. (1969). *Symbolic interactionism: Perspective and method.* Englewood Cliffs, NJ: Prentice-Hall.

- Bodie, G. D., St. Cyr, K., Pence, M., Rold, M., & Honeycutt, J. (2008). Listening competence in initial interactions: Distinguishing between what listening is and what listeners do. *International Journal of Listening, 22*(1), 12-28.

- Bonk, C. J., Lee, M. M., Kou, X., Xu, S., & Sheu, F. R. (2015). Understanding the self-directed online learning preferences, goals, achievements, and challenges of MIT OpenCourseWare subscribers. *Educational Technology & Society, 18*(2), 349-368.

- Bordia, P., Hunt, E., Paulsen, N., Tourish, D., & DiFonzo, N. (2004). Uncertainty during organizational change: Is it all about control? *European Journal of Work and Organizational Psychology, 13*(3), 345-365.

- Borman, W. C., & Motowidlo, S. J. (1993). Expanding the criterion domain to include elements of contextual performance. *Personnel Selection in Organizations*, 71, 98.

- Boud, D. (1995). Enhancing learning through self-assessment. Kogan Page.

- Boud, D., & Middleton, H. (2003). Learning from others at work: Communities of practice and informal learning. *Journal of Workplace Learning, 15*(5), 194-202.

- Boud, D., & Molloy, E. (2013). *Rethinking models of feedback for learning: The challenge of design.* Assessment & Evaluation in Higher Education, 38(6), 698-712.

- Bracken, D. W., Timmreck, C. W., & Church, A. H. (2001). *The handbook of multisource feedback.* Jossey-Bass.

- Brett, J. F., & Atwater, L. E. (2001). 360° feedback: Accuracy, reactions, and perceptions of usefulness. *Journal of Applied Psychology, 86*(5), 930-942.

- Bridges, W. (2009). *Managing transitions: Making the most of change.* Da Capo Press.

- Brinkmann, S., & Kvale, S. (2018). *Doing interviews.* Sage.

- Brookfield, S. (1984). *Self-directed adult learning: A critical paradigm.* Adult Education Quarterly, 35(2), 59-71.

- Brown, J. S., & Duguid, P. (1991). Organizational learning and communities-of-practice: Toward a unified view of working, learning, and innovation. *Organization Science, 2*(1), 40-57.

- Brownell, J. (1987). Listening: Attitudes, principles, and skills. *Journal of Business Communication, 24*(4), 41-54.

- Brun, J. P., & Dugas, N. (2008). An analysis of employee recognition: Perspectives on human resources practices. *The*

References

International Journal of Human Resource Management, 19(4), 716-730.

- Bryan, L. L., & Joyce, C. I. (2005). The 21st-century organization. The McKinsey Quarterly, 3, 24-33.

- Bughin, J., & Chui, M. (2010). The rise of the networked enterprise: Web 2.0 finds its payday. McKinsey Quarterly, 4, 3-8.

- Burgoon, J. K. (1993). Interpersonal expectations, expectancy violations, and emotional communication. Journal of Language and Social Psychology, 12(1-2), 30-48.

- Burgoon, J. K., Birk, T., & Pfau, M. (1989). Nonverbal behaviors, persuasion, and credibility. Human Communication Research, 15(3), 399-421.

- Cameron, K. S., & Lavine, M. (2006). Making the impossible possible: Leading extraordinary performance: The Rocky Flats story. Berrett-Koehler Publishers.

- Candy, P. C. (1991). Self-direction for lifelong learning: A comprehensive guide to theory and practice. Jossey-Bass.

- Candy, P. C. (2002). Lifelong learning and information literacy. US White House Conference on Information Literacy.

- Cardon, P. W. (2010). Using films to learn about the nature of cross-cultural stereotypes in intercultural business communication courses. Business Communication Quarterly, 73(2), 150-165.

- Carrington, M. J., Neville, B. A., & Whitwell, G. J. (2010). Why ethical consumers don't walk their talk: Towards a framework for understanding the gap between the ethical purchase intentions and actual buying behaviour of ethically minded consumers. *Journal of Business Ethics, 97*(1), 139-158.

- Castells, M. (2011). *The rise of the network society: The information age: Economy, society, and culture* (Vol. 1). John Wiley & Sons.

- Chaudhuri, S., & Ghosh, R. (2012). Reverse mentoring: A social exchange tool for keeping the boomers engaged and millennials committed. *Human Resource Development Review, 11*(1), 55-76.

- Chen, Y., Shao, Y., & Wei, Y. (2015). How does organizational structure matter in influencing employee behaviors? *Frontiers in Psychology, 6*, 1176.

- Chevalier, J. A., & Mayzlin, D. (2006). The effect of word of mouth on sales: Online book reviews. *Journal of Marketing Research, 43*(3), 345-354.

- Chung, N., Lee, H., & Rao, H. R. (2016). Exploring the determinants of augmented reality adoption intention: Perspectives from theories of innovation diffusion and uses and gratification. *Journal of Cybersecurity and Privacy, 1*(1), 3-24.

- Cirillo, F. (2006). The Pomodoro Technique: The acclaimed time-management system that has transformed how we work.

- Clark, R. C., & Mayer, R. E. (2016). *E-learning and the science of instruction: Proven guidelines for consumers and designers of multimedia learning*. John Wiley & Sons.

References

- Clark, S. C. (2010). Work/family border theory: A new theory of work/family balance. *Human Relations, 53*(6), 747-770.

- Cohen, G. L., Steele, C. M., & Ross, L. D. (1999). The mentor's dilemma: Providing critical feedback across the racial divide. *Personality and Social Psychology Bulletin, 25*(10), 1302-1318.

- Colquitt, J. A., Conlon, D. E., Wesson, M. J., Porter, C. O., & Ng, K. Y. (2001). Justice at the millennium: a meta-analytic review of 25 years of organizational justice research. *Journal of applied psychology, 86*(3), 425.

- Combs, J., Liu, Y., Hall, A., & Ketchen, D. (2006). How much do high-performance work practices matter? A meta-analysis of their effects on organizational performance. *Personnel Psychology, 59*(3), 501-528.

- Cornelissen, J. (2014). *Corporate communication: A guide to theory and practice.* London: Sage.

- Covey, S. R. (1989). *The 7 habits of highly effective people: Powerful lessons in personal change.* Simon and Schuster.

- Cox, T. H. (1994). *Cultural diversity in organizations: Theory, research, and practice.* Berrett-Koehler Publishers.

- Cox, T., & Blake, S. (1991). Managing cultural diversity: Implications for organizational competitiveness. *Academy of Management Executive, 5*(3), 45-56.

- Craik, J. (2005). *Uniforms exposed: From conformity to transgression.* Berg Publishers.

- Crane, D. (2000). *Fashion and its social agendas: Class, gender, and identity in clothing.* University of Chicago Press.

- Cross, K. P. (1981). Adults as learners. *Increasing participation and facilitating learning.*

- Cummings, J. N. (2004). Work groups, structural diversity, and knowledge sharing in a global organization. *Management Science, 50*(3), 352-364.

- Daft, R. L., & Lengel, R. H. (1986). Organizational information requirements, media richness, and structural design. *Management Science, 32*(5), 554-571.

- Dahl, R. A. (1957). The concept of power. *Behavioral Science, 2*(3), 201-215.

- Dale, K. (2013). *Body/embodiment: Symbolic interaction and the sociology of the body.* Routledge.

- Davidow, M. (2003). Have you heard the word? The effect of word of mouth on perceived justice, satisfaction and repurchase intentions following complaint handling. *Journal of Consumer Satisfaction, Dissatisfaction and Complaining Behavior, 16*, 67-80.

- Davies, P. (2010). On school educational technology leadership. *Management in Education, 24*(2), 55-61.

- De Dreu, C. K. (2008). The virtue and vice of workplace conflict: food for (pessimistic) thought. *Journal of Organizational Behavior, 29*(1), 5-18.

References

- DeChurch, L. A., & Mesmer-Magnus, J. R. (2010). The cognitive underpinnings of effective teamwork: a meta-analysis. *Journal of Applied Psychology, 95*(1), 32.

- Deci, E. L., & Ryan, R. M. (1985). *Intrinsic motivation and self-determination in human behavior*. Plenum.

- Deci, E. L., & Ryan, R. M. (2000). The" what" and" why" of goal pursuits: Human needs and the self-determination of behavior. *Psychological Inquiry, 11*(4), 227-268.

- Deci, E. L., Vallerand, R. J., Pelletier, L. G., & Ryan, R. M. (1991). Motivation and education: The self-determination perspective. *Educational Psychologist, 26*(3&4), 325-346.

- Deming, W. E. (1986). *Out of the crisis*. MIT press.

- Denis, J. L., Langley, A., & Rouleau, L. (2010). The practice of leadership in the messy world of organizations. *Leadership, 6*(1), 67-88.

- DeNisi, A. S., & Kluger, A. N. (2000). Feedback effectiveness: Can 360-degree appraisals be improved? *Academy of Management Executive, 14*(1), 129-139.

- DeNisi, A. S., & Pritchard, R. D. (2006). Performance appraisal, performance management and improving individual performance: A motivational framework. *Management and Organization Review, 2*(2), 253-277.

- Denison, D. R. (1990). Corporate culture and organizational effectiveness. *John Wiley & Sons*.

- Derlega, V. J., & Chaikin, A. L. (1977). *Privacy and self-disclosure in social relationships.* Journal of Social Issues, 33(3), 102-115.

- Detert, J. R., & Burris, E. R. (2007). Leadership behavior and employee voice: Is the door really open? *Academy of Management Journal, 50*(4), 869-884.

- DeVos, A., & Soens, N. (2008). Protean attitude and career success: The mediating role of self-management. *Journal of Vocational Behavior, 73*(3), 449-456.

- DiFonzo, N., & Bordia, P. (1998). A tale of two corporations: Managing uncertainty during organizational change. *Human Resource Management, 37*(3-4), 295-303.

- Dipboye, R. L., & de Pontbriand, R. (1981). Correlates of employee reactions to performance appraisals and appraisal systems. *Journal of Applied Psychology, 66*(2), 248-251.

- Dirks, K. T., & Ferrin, D. L. (2001). The role of trust in organizational settings. *Organization Science, 12*(4), 450-467.

- Dixon, M., Freeman, K., & Toman, N. (2010). Stop trying to delight your customers. *Harvard Business Review, 88*(7/8), 116-122.

- Doran, G. T. (1981). There's a S.M.A.R.T. way to write management's goals and objectives. *Management Review, 70*(11), 35-36.

- Driscoll, M. (2002). *Blended learning: Let's get beyond the hype.* E-learning, 1(4), 1-4.

References

- Drucker, P. (1999). *Managing oneself.* Harvard Business Review, 77(2), 64-74.

- Drucker, P. F. (1954). *The practice of management.* Harper & Row.

- Drucker, P. F. (1999). *Knowledge-worker productivity: The biggest challenge.* California management review, 41(2), 79-94.

- Duhigg, C. (2012). *The power of habit: Why we do what we do in life and business.* Random House.

- Duke, C. (2002). *Lifelong learning: A political necessity?.* NIACE.

- Dunning, D., Heath, C., & Suls, J. M. (2004). Flawed self-assessment: Implications for health, education, and the workplace. *Psychological Science in the Public Interest, 5*(3), 69-106.

- Dunning, D., Johnson, K., Ehrlinger, J., & Kruger, J. (2003). Why people fail to recognize their own incompetence. *Current Directions in Psychological Science, 12*(3), 83-87.

- Dweck, C. S. (2006). *Mindset: The new psychology of success.* Random House.

- Dyer, W. G., Dyer, W. G. Jr., & Dyer, J. H. (2007). *Team building: Proven strategies for improving team performance.* San Francisco, CA: Jossey-Bass.

- East, R., Hammond, K., & Lomax, W. (2007). Measuring the impact of positive and negative word of mouth on brand purchase probability. *International Journal of Research in Marketing, 25*(3), 215-224.

- Eby, L. T., Allen, T. D., & Scandura, T. A. (2006). The relationship between mentoring and career outcomes: A multiple mentoring perspective. *Journal of Vocational Behavior, 68*(2), 164-176.

- Eby, L. T., Allen, T. D., Evans, S. C., Ng, T., & Dubois, D. (2008). Does mentoring matter? A multidisciplinary meta-analysis comparing mentored and non-mentored individuals. *Journal of Vocational Behavior, 72*(2), 254-267.

- Edmondson, A. (1999). Psychological safety and learning behavior in work teams. *Administrative Science Quarterly, 44*(2), 350-383.

- Edmondson, A. (1999). Psychological safety and learning behavior in work teams. *Administrative Science Quarterly, 44*(2), 350-383.

- Edmondson, A. (2003). Speaking up in the operating room: How team leaders promote learning in interdisciplinary action teams. *Journal of Management Studies, 40*(6), 1419-1452.

- Edwards, M. R., & Ewen, A. J. (1996). *360° feedback: The powerful new model for employee assessment & performance improvement.* AMACOM.

- Eisenbeiss, S. A., Knippenberg, D. V., & Boerner, S. (2008). Transformational leadership and team innovation: Integrating team climate principles. *Journal of Applied Psychology, 93*(6), 1438-1446.

References

- Eisenberg, N., & Miller, P. A. (1987). The relation of empathy to prosocial and related behaviors. *Psychological Bulletin, 101*(1), 91-119.

- Ellis, A. (2001). Overcoming destructive beliefs, feelings, and behaviors: New directions for rational emotive behavior therapy. Prometheus Books.

- Entwistle, J. (2000). *The fashioned body: Fashion, dress, and modern social theory*. Polity.

- Eppler, M. J., & Mengis, J. (2004). The concept of information overload: A review of literature from organization science, accounting, marketing, MIS, and related disciplines. *The Information Society, 20*(5), 325-344.

- Eppler, M. J., & Mengis, J. (2004). The concept of information overload: A review of literature from organization science, accounting, marketing, MIS, and related disciplines. *The Information Society, 20*(5), 325-344.

- Eraut, M. (2004). Informal learning in the workplace. *Studies in Continuing Education, 26*(2), 247-273.

- Eva, K. W., & Regehr, G. (2005). Self-assessment in the health professions: A reformulation and research agenda. *Academic Medicine, 80*(10), S46-S54.

- Eva, K. W., & Regehr, G. (2005). Self-assessment in the health professions: A reformulation and research agenda. *Academic Medicine, 80*(10), S46-S54.

- Fairhurst, G. T., & Sarr, R. A. (1996). *The art of framing: Managing the language of leadership*. San Francisco: Jossey-Bass.

- Fast, N. J., Burris, E. R., & Bartel, C. A. (2014). Managing to stay in the dark: Managerial self-efficacy, ego defensiveness, and the aversion to employee voice. *Academy of Management Journal, 57*(4), 1013-1034.

- Fehr, R., & Gelfand, M. J. (2010). When apologies work: How matching apology components to victims' self-construals facilitates forgiveness. *Organizational Behavior and Human Decision Processes, 113*(1), 37-50.

- Festinger, L., Schachter, S., & Back, K. (1950). *Social pressures in informal groups: A study of human factors in housing*. Harper.

- Festinger, L., Schachter, S., & Back, K. (1950). *Social pressures in informal groups: A study of human factors in housing*. Stanford University Press.

- Field, J. (2001). Lifelong education. *International Journal of Lifelong Education, 20*(1-2), 3-15.

- Fisher, R., & Ury, W. (1981). *Getting to yes: Negotiating agreement without giving in*. Penguin.

- Forester, J. (1999). *The deliberative practitioner: Encouraging participatory planning processes*. MIT press.

- Forsythe, S. M. (1990). Effect of applicant's clothing on interviewer's decision to hire. *Journal of Applied Social Psychology, 20*(19), 1579-1595.

References

- French, J. R., & Raven, B. (1959). The bases of social power. *Group dynamics*, 150-167.

- Friedman, T. L. (2005). *The world is flat: A brief history of the twenty-first century*. Farrar, Straus, and Giroux.

- Fullan, M. (2001). *Leading in a culture of change*. Jossey-Bass.

- Fullan, M. (2007). *The new meaning of educational change* (4th ed.). Teachers College Press.

- Gabarro, J. J. (1978). The development of trust, influence, and expectations. In A. G. Athos & J. J. Gabarro (Eds.), *Interpersonal behavior: Communication and understanding in relationships* (pp. 290-303). Prentice-Hall.

- Gartner (2018). *Survey Analysis: Customer Experience Innovation 2017 – A Midsize Enterprise Peer Insights Perspective*. Gartner, Inc.

- Garvin, D. A. (1993). Building a learning organization. *Harvard Business Review, 71*(4), 78-91.

- Gibbs, G. (1988). *Learning by doing: A guide to teaching and learning methods*. FEU.

- Gillis, T. (2011). *The IABC handbook of organizational communication: A guide to internal communication, public relations, marketing, and leadership*. San Francisco: Jossey-Bass.

- Gilly, M. C., & Gelb, B. D. (1982). Post-purchase consumer processes and the complaining consumer. *Journal of Consumer Research, 9*(3), 323-328.

- Girard, J. P., & Pinar, M. (2019). Improving salesperson's adaptive selling and active listening through manager's feedback and supervision. *Journal of Business & Industrial Marketing, 34*(4), 754-769.

- Glaveanu, V. P., de Saint-Laurent, C., & Wegener, C. (2019). Making the familiar unfamiliar: An investigation of the role of clothing in cultural encounters. *Culture & Psychology, 25*(1), 3-21.

- Goetzel, R. Z., Long, S. R., Ozminkowski, R. J., Hawkins, K., Wang, S., & Lynch, W. (2004). Health, absence, disability, and presenteeism cost estimates of certain physical and mental health conditions affecting U.S. employers. *Journal of Occupational and Environmental Medicine, 46*(4), 398-412.

- Goldberg, L. R. (1990). An alternative "description of personality": The Big-Five factor structure. *Journal of Personality and Social Psychology, 59*(6), 1216-1229.

- Goldstein, I. L., & Ford, J. K. (2002). *Training in organizations: Needs assessment, development, and evaluation.* Wadsworth.

- Goleman, D. (1995). *Emotional intelligence.* Bantam Books.

- Goodhue, D. L., & Thompson, R. L. (1995). Task-technology fit and individual performance. *MIS Quarterly*, 213-236.

References

- Gordon, T. (1977). *Leader effectiveness training, L.E.T: The no-lose way to release the productive potential of people*. Putnam Publishing Group.

- Gotsi, M., Andriopoulos, C., Lewis, M. W., & Ingram, A. E. (2010). Managing creatives: Paradoxical approaches to identity regulation. *Human Relations, 63*(6), 781-805.

- Grandey, A. A., Dickter, D. N., & Sin, H. P. (2004). The customer is not always right: Customer aggression and emotion regulation of service employees. *Journal of Organizational*

- Granovetter, M. S. (1973). The strength of weak ties. *American Journal of Sociology, 78*(6), 1360-1380.

- Greenberg, P. (2010). *CRM at the speed of light: Social CRM strategies, tools, and techniques for engaging your customers*. McGraw Hill Professional.

- Greenhaus, J. H., & Beutell, N. J. (1985). Sources and conflict between work and family roles. *Academy of Management Review, 10*(1), 76-88.

- Greenhaus, J. H., Collins, K. M., Singh, R., & Parasuraman, S. (2003). Work and family influences on departure from public accounting. *Journal of Vocational Behavior, 63*(3), 447-464.

- Gross, J. J. (2002). Emotion regulation: Affective, cognitive, and social consequences. *Psychophysiology, 39*(3), 281-291.

- Grunig, J. E. (1992). *Excellence in public relations and communication management*. Hillsdale, NJ: Lawrence Erlbaum Associates.

- Gudykunst, W. B. (2004). *Bridging differences: Effective group communication*. Thousand Oaks, CA: Sage.

- Gupta, A. K., & Singhal, A. (1993). Managing human resources for innovation and creativity. *Research-Technology Management, 36*(3), 41-48.

- Guzzo, R. A., & Dickson, M. W. (1996). Teams in organizations: Recent research on performance and effectiveness. *Annual review of psychology, 47*(1), 307-338.

- Hall, D. T. (2004). The protean career: A quarter-century journey. *Journal of Vocational Behavior, 65*(1), 1-13.

- Hall, E. T. (1976). *Beyond culture*. Anchor Press.

- Hannan, M. T., & Freeman, J. (1984). Structural inertia and organizational change. *American Sociological Review, 49*(2), 149-164.

- Harrison, D. A. (1995). Volunteer motivation and attendance decisions: Competitive theory testing in multiple samples from a homeless shelter. *Journal of Applied Psychology, 80*(3), 371-385.

- Hartel, C. E., Ashkanasy, N. M., & Zerbe, W. J. (1999). *Emotions in the workplace: Research, theory, and practice*. Quorum Books.

- Harter, J. K., Schmidt, F. L., & Hayes, T. L. (2002). Business-unit-level relationship between employee satisfaction, employee engagement, and business outcomes: A meta-analysis. *Journal of Applied Psychology, 87*(2), 268.

References

- Hattie, J., & Timperley, H. (2007). The power of feedback. *Review of Educational Research, 77*(1), 81-112.

- Hausknecht, J. P., Trevor, C. O., & Howard, M. J. (2009). Unit-level voluntary turnover rates and customer service quality: Implications of group cohesiveness, newcomer concentration, and size. *Journal of Applied Psychology, 94*(4), 1068.

- Hayes, D. K. (2008). *Human resources management in the hospitality industry*. John Wiley & Sons.

- Heath, R. L. (1997). *Strategic issues management: Organizations and public policy challenges*. Thousand Oaks, CA: Sage.

- Heckscher, C., & Donnellon, A. (1994). *The post-bureaucratic organization: New perspectives on organizational change*. Sage.

- Hemp, P. (2004). Presenteeism: At work—But out of it. *Harvard Business Review, 82*(10), 49-58.

- Herzberg, F. (1959). The motivation to work. *John Wiley & Sons.*

- Herzberg, F. (1968). *One more time: How do you motivate employees?* Harvard Business Review.

- Heskett, J. L., Jones, T. O., Loveman, G. W., Sasser, W. E., & Schlesinger, L. A. (2008). Putting the service-profit chain to work. *Harvard Business Review, 72*(2), 164-174.

- Heskett, J. L., Sasser Jr, W. E., & Schlesinger, L. A. (1997). *The service-profit chain*. The Free Press.

- Higgins, M. C., & Kram, K. E. (2001). Reconceptualizing mentoring at work: A developmental network perspective. *Academy of Management Review, 26*(2), 264-288.

- Hilbrecht, M., Shaw, S. M., Johnson, L. C., & Andrey, J. (2008). 'I'm home for the kids': Contradictory implications for work–life balance of teleworking mothers. *Gender, Work & Organization, 15*(5), 454-476.

- Hinds, P. J., Neeley, T. B., & Cramton, C. D. (2014). Language as a lightning rod: Power contests, emotion regulation, and subgroup dynamics in global teams. *Journal of International Business Studies, 45*(5), 536-561.

- Hines, P., & Rich, N. (1997). The seven value stream mapping tools. *International Journal of Operations & Production Management, 17*(1), 46-64.

- Hollander, A. (1994). *Sex and suits: The evolution of modern dress*. Kodansha America.

- Holt, D. B. (2002). Why do brands cause trouble? A dialectical theory of consumer culture and branding. *Journal of Consumer Research, 29*(1), 70-90.

- Holton III, E. F., Bates, R. A., & Ruona, W. E. (2000). Development of a generalized learning transfer system inventory. *Human Resource Development Quarterly, 11*(4), 333-360.

- House, R. J. (1971). A path-goal theory of leader effectiveness. *Administrative Science Quarterly, 16*(3), 321-339.

References

- Howlett, N., Pine, K. J., Orakçıoğlu, I., & Fletcher, B. C. (2013). The influence of clothing on first impressions: Rapid and positive responses to minor changes in male attire. *Journal of Fashion Marketing and Management: An International Journal, 17*(1), 38-48.

- Huang, M. H., & Rust, R. T. (2018). Artificial intelligence in service. *Journal of Service Research, 21*(2), 155-172.

- Hug, T. (2005). Micro learning and narration: Exploring possibilities of utilization of narrations and storytelling for the designing of "micro units" and didactical micro-learning arrangements. *Media in Foreign Language Teaching and Learning, 38*, 103-114.

- Hughes, F. T. (2002). Dress codes and grooming. *Employment Discrimination Law, 35*(4), 27-38.

- Hunton, J. E., & Gold, A. (2010). A field experiment comparing the outcomes of three fraud brainstorming procedures: Nominal group, round robin, and open discussion. *The Accounting Review, 85*(3), 911-935.

- Huselid, M. A. (1995). The impact of human resource management practices on turnover, productivity, and corporate financial performance. *Academy of Management Journal, 38*(3), 635-672.

- Huselid, M. A. (1995). The impact of human resource management practices on turnover, productivity, and corporate financial performance. *Academy of Management Journal, 38*(3), 635-672.

- Ibarra, H. (1999). Provisional selves: Experimenting with image and identity in professional adaptation. *Administrative Science Quarterly, 44*(4), 764-791.

- Ilgen, D. R., Fisher, C. D., & Taylor, M. S. (1979). Consequences of individual feedback on behavior in organizations. *Journal of Applied Psychology, 64*(4), 349-371.

- Jacobides, M. G. (2019). *Rethinking the corporation's redesign.* MIT Sloan Management Review.

- Jarvis, P. (2009). *Lifelong learning: A social ambiguity.* In *Lifelong learning & the learning society* (Vol. 1, pp. 1-21). Routledge.

- Jehn, K. A. (1995). A multimethod examination of the benefits and detriments of intragroup conflict. *Administrative Science Quarterly, 40*(2), 256-282.

- Jenkins, A., & Mostafa, T. (2015). The effects of learning on wellbeing for older adults in England. *Ageing & Society, 35*(10), 2053-2070.

- Johnson, A. H., & Ng, E. S. (2016). Money matters: Recommendations for financial literacy education for transgender and gender non-conforming individuals. *Gender, Work & Organization, 23*(2), 183-200.

- Johnson, W. B. (2002). *The intentional mentor: Strategies and guidelines for the practice of mentoring.* Professional Psychology: Research and Practice, 33(1), 88-96.

References

- Jordan, P. J., & Troth, A. C. (2004). Managing emotions during team problem solving: Emotional intelligence and conflict resolution. *Human Performance, 17*(2), 195-218.

- Joseph, N. M., & Alex, N. (1972). *The uniform: A sociological perspective.* Transaction Publishers.

- Joyce, B. R., & Showers, B. (2002). *Student achievement through staff development.* Association for Supervision and Curriculum Development.

- Judge, T. A., Thoresen, C. J., Bono, J. E., & Patton, G. K. (2001). The job satisfaction-job performance relationship: A qualitative and quantitative review. *Psychological Bulletin, 127*(3), 376.

- Kacmar, K. M., & Ferris, G. R. (1991). Perceptions of organizational politics scale (POPS): Development and construct validation. *Educational and Psychological Measurement, 51*(1), 193-205.

- Kegan, R. (1982). *The evolving self: Problem and process in human development.* Harvard University Press.

- Keller, K. L. (1993). Conceptualizing, measuring, and managing customer-based brand equity. *Journal of Marketing, 57*(1), 1-22.

- Kerres, M., & Witt, C. D. (2003). A didactical framework for the design of blended learning arrangements. *Journal of Educational Media, 28*(2-3), 101-113.

- Kindley, R. (2002). Scenario-based e-learning: A step beyond traditional e-learning. *Learning Circuits, American Society for Training and Development (ASTD).*

References

- Kirkpatrick, D. L., & Kirkpatrick, J. D. (2006). *Evaluating training programs*. Berrett-Koehler Publishers.

- Klein, C., DiazGranados, D., Salas, E., Le, H., Burke, C. S., Lyons, R., & Goodwin, G. F. (2009). Does team building work? *Small Group Research, 40*(2), 181-222.

- Kluger, A. N., & DeNisi, A. (1996). The effects of feedback interventions on performance: A historical review, a meta-analysis, and a preliminary feedback intervention theory. *Psychological Bulletin, 119*(2), 254-284.

- Kniffin, K. M., Narayanan, J., Anseel, F., Antonakis, J., Ashford, S. P., Bakker, A. B., ... & Vugt, M. V. (2021). COVID-19 and the workplace: Imp

- Knowles, M. S. (1980). *The modern practice of adult education: From pedagogy to andragogy*. Follett.

- Knowles, M. S., Holton III, E. F., & Swanson, R. A. (2014). *The adult learner: The definitive classic in adult education and human resource development* (8th ed.). Routledge.

- Knowles, M. S., Holton III, E. F., & Swanson, R. A. (2014). *The adult learner*. Routledge.

- Kolb, D. A. (1984). *Experiential learning: Experience as the source of learning and development*. Prentice-Hall.

- Kotter, J. P. (1995). Leading change: Why transformation efforts fail. *Harvard Business Review, 73*(2), 59-67.

References

- Kotter, J. P. (1996). Leading change. *Harvard Business Review, 73*(2), 59-67.

- Kotter, J. P., & Schlesinger, L. A. (2008). Choosing strategies for change. *Harvard Business Review, 86*(7/8), 130-139.

- KPMG (2020). *The truth about customer loyalty.* KPMG International.

- Kram, K. E. (1985). *Mentoring at work: Developmental relationships in organizational life.* Scott, Foresman.

- Kraus, M. W., & Mendes, W. B. (2014). Sartorial symbols of social class elicit class-consistent behavioral and physiological responses: A dyadic approach. *Journal of Experimental Psychology: General, 143*(6), 2330-2340.

- Kraut, R. E., Egido, C., & Galegher, J. (1988). Patterns of contact and communication in scientific research collaboration. In *Proceedings of the 1988 ACM conference on Computer-supported cooperative work* (pp. 1-12).

- Kwintessential (2010). Dress and behavior as cultural signifiers. *Cultural Awareness International, 5*(2), 12-17.

- Kwon, Y. H. (1994). Feeling toward one's clothing and self-perception of emotion, sociability, and work competency

- novelty: A case in clothing selection. *Clothing and Textiles Research Journal, 12*(4), 31-38.

- Laal, M., & Salamati, P. (2012). Lifelong learning; why do we need it? *Procedia-Social and Behavioral Sciences, 31*, 399-403.

- Labrecque, L. I., Markos, E., & Milne, G. R. (2011). Online personal branding: Processes, challenges, and implications. *Journal of Interactive Marketing, 25*(1), 37-50.

- Lacey, R., & Suh, J. (2010). Customer satisfaction and loyalty: The critical elements of service quality. *Total Quality Management, 21*(10), 1127-1140.

- Laros, F. J. M., & Steenkamp, J.-B. E. M. (2005). Emotions in consumer behavior: hierarchical approach. *Journal of Business Research, 58*(10), 1437-1445.

- Lave, J., & Wenger, E. (1991). Situated learning: Legitimate peripheral participation. Cambridge University Press.

- Lawler, E. E. (1971). *Pay and organizational effectiveness: A psychological view.* McGraw-Hill.

- Lawler, E. E. (1971). *Pay and organizational effectiveness: A psychological view.* McGraw-Hill.

- Lemon, K. N., White, T. B., & Winer, R. S. (2002). Dynamic customer relationship management: Incorporating future considerations into the service retention decision. *Journal of Marketing, 66*(1), 1-14.

- Leonardi, P. M., & Treem, J. W. (2012). Knowledge management technology as a stage for strategic self-presentation: Implications for knowledge sharing in organizations. *Information and Organization, 22*(1), 37-59.

- Leonardi, P. M., Huysman, M., & Steinfield, C. (2013). Enterprise social media: Definition, history, and prospects for the study of

References

social technologies in organizations. *Journal of Computer-Mediated Communication, 19*(1), 1-19.

- Lewin, K. (1947). Frontiers in group dynamics. *Human Relations, 1*(1), 5-41.

- Likert, R. (1961). *New patterns of management.* McGraw-Hill.

- Locke, E. A., & Latham, G. P. (1984). *Goal setting: A motivational technique that works.* Prentice Hall.

- Locke, E. A., & Latham, G. P. (1990). *A theory of goal setting & task performance.* Prentice Hall.

- Locke, E. A., & Latham, G. P. (2002). Building a practically useful theory of goal setting and task motivation: A 35-year odyssey. *American Psychologist, 57*(9), 705.

- Locke, E. A., & Latham, G. P. (2006). New directions in goal-setting theory. *Current Directions in Psychological Science, 15*(5), 265-268.

- London, M. (1983). Toward a theory of career motivation. *Academy of Management Review, 8*(4), 620-630.

- London, M. (1995). *Self and interpersonal insight: How people gain an understanding of themselves and others in organizations.* Oxford University Press.

- London, M. (2003). *Job feedback: Giving, seeking, and using feedback for performance improvement.* Lawrence Erlbaum Associates Publishers.

- London, M., & Smither, J. W. (1995). Can multi-source feedback change perceptions of goal accomplishment, self-evaluations, and performance-related outcomes? Theory-based applications and directions for research. *Personnel Psychology, 48*(4), 803-839.

- London, M., & Smither, J. W. (2002). Feedback orientation, feedback culture, and the longitudinal performance process. *Human Resource Management Review, 12*(1), 81-100.

- Lukes, S. (1974). *Power: A radical view*. Macmillan.

- Lundqvist, A., Liljander, V., Gummerus, J., & van Riel, A. (2013). The impact of storytelling on the consumer brand experience: The case of a firm-originated story. *Journal of Brand Management, 20*(4), 283-297.

- Maklan, S., Klaus, P., & Peacock, A. (2015). Customer Experience: Are We Measuring the Right Things?. *International Journal of Market Research, 57*(6), 855-870.

- Mann, S., & Holdsworth, L. (2003). The psychological impact of teleworking: Stress, emotions and health. *New Technology, Work and Employment, 18*(3), 196-211.

- Marr, B. (2016). *How big data is changing the way we do business*. Bernard Marr & Co.

- Martin, K. D. (2018). The role of privacy in marketing. *Journal of the Academy of Marketing Science, 46*(2), 205-221.

- Masten, A. S. (2001). Ordinary magic: Resilience processes in development. *American Psychologist, 56*(3), 227.

References

- Mathieu, J., Maynard, M. T., Rapp, T., & Gilson, L. (2008). Team effectiveness 1997-2007: A review of recent advancements and a glimpse into the future. *Journal of management, 34*(3), 410-476.

- Maurer, T. J. (2001). Career-relevant learning and development, worker age, and beliefs about self-efficacy for development. *Journal of Management, 27*(2), 123-140.

- Maxham III, J. G. (2001). Service recovery's influence on consumer satisfaction, positive word-of-mouth, and purchase intentions. *Journal of Business Research, 54*(1), 11-24.

- Maxham III, J. G., & Netemeyer, R. G. (2002). A longitudinal study of complaining customers' evaluations of multiple service failures and recovery efforts. *Journal of Marketing, 66*(4), 57-71.

- Mayer, R. C., Davis, J. H., & Schoorman, F. D. (1995). An integrative model of organizational trust. *Academy of Management Review, 20*(3), 709-734.

- McCormick, K. (2016). Personalization vs. privacy: A delicate balance. *Financial Brand*.

- McGregor, D. (1960). *The human side of enterprise*. McGraw-Hill.

- Mehrabian, A. (1971). *Silent messages*. Wadsworth.

- Mehrabian, A. (1972). *Nonverbal communication*. Aldine-Atherton.

- Mental Health Commission of Canada. (2012). *Psychological health and safety in the workplace: Prevention, promotion, and guidance to staged implementation*. BNQ & CSA Group.

- Merriam, S. B., & Bierema, L. L. (2014). *Adult learning: Linking theory and practice*. Jossey-Bass.

- Meyer, C., & Schwager, A. (2007). Understanding customer experience. *Harvard Business Review, 85*(2), 116-126.

- Michael, W. B. (2006). Clothing conformity and group cohesiveness. *Journal of Social Psychology, 62*(1), 29-33.

- Miller, K. (1997). *Dress and gender: Making and meaning*. Berg Publishers.

- Milliken, F. J., Morrison, E. W., & Hewlin, P. F. (2003). An exploratory study of employee silence: Issues that employees don't communicate upward and why. *Journal of Management Studies, 40*(6), 1453-1476.

- Mitchell, R. (2002). The impact of individual and managerial factors on salespeople's contribution to marketing intelligence activities. *International Journal of Research in Marketing, 19*(4), 323-338.

- Mohr, J., & Nevin, J. R. (1990). Communication strategies in marketing channels: A theoretical perspective. *Journal of Marketing, 54*(4), 36-51.

- Moon, J. A. (2004). A handbook of reflective and experiential learning: Theory and practice. Routledge.

References

- Moon, J. A. (2004). A handbook of reflective and experiential learning: Theory and practice. Routledge.

- Moore, C. W. (2014). *The mediation process: Practical strategies for resolving conflict*. John Wiley & Sons.

- Morgan, N. A., & Rego, L. L. (2006). The value of different customer satisfaction and loyalty metrics in predicting business performance. *Marketing Science, 25*(5), 426-439.

- Morgan, N. A., & Rego, L. L. (2006). The value of different customer satisfaction and loyalty metrics in predicting business performance. *Marketing Science, 25*(5), 426-439.

- Morisano, D., Hirsh, J. B., Peterson, J. B., Pihl, R. O., & Shore, B. M. (2010). Setting, elaborating, and reflecting on personal goals improves academic performance. *Journal of Applied Psychology, 95*(2), 255-264.

- Morrison, E. W., & Milliken, F. J. (2000). Organizational silence: A barrier to change and development in a pluralistic world. *The Academy of Management Review, 25*(4), 706-725.

- Morrison, R. (2004). Informal relationships in the workplace: Associations with job satisfaction, organisational commitment and turnover intentions. *New Zealand Journal of Psychology, 33*(3), 114-128.

- Morrison, R. (2004). Informal relationships in the workplace: Associations with job satisfaction, organisational commitment and turnover intentions. *New Zealand Journal of Psychology, 33*(3), 114-128.

- Mount, M. K. (1983). Implications of research on rating distortion for performance appraisal. *Organizational Behavior and Human Performance, 31*(1), 42-60.

- Murphy, N. A., Hall, J. A., & Colvin, C. R. (2003). Accurate intelligence assessments in social interactions: Mediators and gender effects. *Journal of Personality, 71*(3), 465-493.

- Myers, I. B., & McCaulley, M. H. (1985). *Manual: A guide to the development and use of the Myers-Briggs type indicator.* Consulting Psychologists Press.

- Myers, I. B., & McCaulley, M. H. (1995). *Manual: A guide to the development and use of the Myers-Briggs Type Indicator.* Consulting Psychologists Press.

- Nankervis, A. R., & Compton, R. L. (2006). Performance management: Theory in practice? *Asia Pacific Journal of Human Resources, 44*(1), 83-101.

- Ngai, E. W., Xiu, L., & Chau, D. C. (2009). Application of data mining techniques in customer relationship management: A literature review and classification. *Expert Systems with Applications, 36*(2), 2592-2602.

- Nichols, R. G. (1957). Listening is a 10 part skill. *Sharing Ideas, 3*(4), 11-16.

- Nicol, D. J., & Macfarlane-Dick, D. (2006). Formative assessment and self-regulated learning: A model and seven principles of good feedback practice. *Studies in Higher Education, 31*(2), 199-218.

References

- Nippert-Eng, C. E. (1996). *Home and work: Negotiating boundaries through everyday life*. University of Chicago Press.

- Noe, R. A. (2010). Employee training and development (5th ed.). McGraw-Hill.

- Nonaka, I., & Takeuchi, H. (1995). *The knowledge-creating company: How Japanese companies create the dynamics of innovation*. Oxford University Press.

- Ohno, T. (1988). *Toyota production system: Beyond large-scale production*. Productivity Press.

- Oliver, R. L. (1997). Satisfaction: A behavioral perspective on the consumer. *McGraw-Hill*.

- Opie, T. (1998). Representing identities: Dress and the construction of a public identity. *Discourse: Studies in the Cultural Politics of Education, 19*(1), 67-78.

- Oreg, S. (2003). Resistance to change: Developing an individual differences measure. *Journal of Applied Psychology, 88*(4), 680-693.

- Osborne, M. (2003). Increasing or widening participation in higher education?—A European overview. *European Journal of Education, 38*(1), 5-24.

- Pace, C. R. (2004). Measuring the quality of student effort. *Current Issues in Higher Education, 2*, 10-16.

- Pantano, E., Rese, A., & Baier, D. (2017). Enhancing the online decision-making process by using augmented reality: A two country comparison of youth markets. *Journal of Retailing and Consumer Services, 38*, 81-95.

- Parasuraman, A., Zeithaml, V. A., & Berry, L. L. (1985). A conceptual model of service quality and its implications for future research. *Journal of Marketing, 49*(4), 41-50.

- Parasuraman, A., Zeithaml, V. A., & Berry, L. L. (1988). SERVQUAL: A multiple-item scale for measuring consumer perceptions of service quality. *Journal of Retailing, 64*(1), 12.

- Parry, K. W., & Thompson, K. (2007). *Distinguishing between leadership development and management training: An exploratory investigation*. University of Western Australia.

- Peluchette, J. V., & Karl, K. (2007). The impact of workplace attire on employee self-perceptions. *Human Resource Development Quarterly, 18*(3), 345-360.

- Peppers, D., & Rogers, M. (1997). *Enterprise one to one: Tools for competing in the interactive age*. Currency Doubleday.

- Peppers, D., & Rogers, M. (2010). *Managing customer relationships: A strategic framework*. John Wiley & Sons.

- Peterson, R. A., Balasubramanian, S., & Bronnenberg, B. J. (1997). Exploring the implications of the Internet for consumer marketing. *Journal of the Academy of Marketing Science, 25*(4), 329-346.

- Petrilli, C. M., Saint S., & Jennings, J. J. (2020). Understanding the specter of the coronavirus disease 2019. *The Journal of Hospital Infection, 105*(2), 176-178.

References

- Pfeffer, J. (1981). *Power in organizations*. Pitman.

- Pfeffer, J. (1994). Competitive advantage through people: Unleashing the power of the workforce. *Harvard Business Press*.

- Phillips, J. J. (1996). *ROI: The search for best practices*. Training & Development, 50(2), 42-47.

- Pine, K. J. (2014). *Mind what you wear: The psychology of fashion*. CreateSpace Independent Publishing Platform.

- Porter, M. E. (1980). Competitive strategy: Techniques for analyzing industries and competitors. *Free Press*.

- Porter, M. E., & Heppelmann, J. E. (2014). How smart, connected products are transforming competition. *Harvard Business Review, 92*(11), 64-88.

- Postrel, V. (2003). *The substance of style: How the rise of aesthetic value is remaking commerce, culture, and consciousness*. HarperCollins.

- Prahalad, C. K., & Ramaswamy, V. (2004). Co-creation experiences: The next practice in value creation. *Journal of Interactive Marketing, 18*(3), 5-14.

- Pratt, M. G., & Rafaeli, A. (1997). Organizational dress as a symbol of multilayered social identities. *Academy of Management Journal, 40*(4), 862-898.

- Pulakos, E. D., Arad, S., Donovan, M. A., & Plamondon, K. E. (2000). Adaptability in the workplace: Development of a taxonomy of adaptive performance. *Journal of Applied Psychology, 85*(4), 612.

- PwC (2018). *Experience is everything: Here's how to get it right.* PwC's Global Consumer Insights Survey.

- Quinn, R. W., & Dutton, J. E. (2005). Coordination as energy-in-conversation. *Academy of Management Review, 30*(1), 36-57.

- Rafaeli, A., & Pratt, M. G. (1993). Tailored meanings: On the meaning and impact of organizational dress. *Academy of Management Review, 18*(1), 32-55.

- Rafaeli, A., Dutton, J., Harquail, C. V., & Mackie-Lewis, S. (1997). Navigating by attire: The use of dress by female administrative employees. *Academy of Management Journal, 40*(1), 9-45.

- Ragins, B. R., & Kram, K. E. (2007). *The handbook of mentoring at work: Theory, research, and practice.* Sage.

- Rahim, M. A. (1983). A measure of styles of handling interpersonal conflict. *The Academy of Management Journal, 26*(2), 368-376.

- Rahim, M. A. (2002). Toward a theory of managing organizational conflict. *The International Journal of Conflict Management, 13*(3), 206-235.

- Rath, T. (2007). *StrengthsFinder 2.0.* Gallup Press.

- Rautalinko, E., & Lisper, H. O. (2004). Effects of training reflective listening in a corporate setting. *Journal of Business and Psychology, 18*(3), 281-299.

References

- Ravazzani, S. (2016). Exploring internal crisis communication in multicultural environments. *Journal of Communication Management, 20*(3), 267-282.

- Reichheld, F. F. (2003). The one number you need to grow. *Harvard Business Review, 81*(12), 46-54.

- Reichheld, F. F., & Sasser, W. E. (1990). Zero defections: Quality comes to services. *Harvard Business Review, 68*(5), 105-111.

- Riggio, R. E. (1986). Assessment of basic social skills. *Journal of Personality and Social Psychology, 51*(3), 649-660.

- Riggio, R. E. (2003). *Introduction to industrial/organizational psychology*. Pearson/Prentice Hall.

- Riggio, R. E., Riggio, H. R., Salinas, C., & Cole, E. J. (2003). The role of social and emotional communication skills in leader emergence and effectiveness. *Group Dynamics: Theory, Research, and Practice, 7*(2), 83-103.

- Rippin, A. (2012). The Qur'an and the hijab: Exploring the textual foundation of wearing the veil. *Gender and Development, 20*(3), 517-530.

- Rizzo, J. R., House, R. J., & Lirtzman, S. I. (1970). Role conflict and ambiguity in complex organizations. *Administrative Science Quarterly, 15*(2), 150-163.

- Roach-Higgins, M. E., & Eicher, J. B. (1992). Dress and identity. *Clothing and Textiles Research Journal, 10*(4), 1-8.

- Robbins, S. P., & Judge, T. A. (2018). *Organizational behavior.* Pearson.

- Roberts, G. E. (2003). Employee performance appraisal system participation: A technique that works. *Public Personnel Management, 32*(1), 89-98.

- Robson, L. S., Clarke, J. A., Clegg, C. W., & Hague, G. (2005). The effectiveness of occupational health and safety management system interventions: A systematic review. *Safety Science, 43*(3), 171-212.

- Rock, D. (2008). SCARF: A brain-based model for collaborating with and influencing others. *NeuroLeadership Journal, 1*(1), 1-9.

- Roethlisberger, F. J., & Dickson, W. J. (1939). *Management and the worker.* Harvard University Press.

- Rogers, C. R. (1951). *Client-centered therapy: Its current practice, implications, and theory.* Houghton Mifflin.

- Rogers, C. R., & Farson, R. E. (1957). Active listening. *Industrial Relations Center of the University of Chicago.*

- Rogers, P. C. (2001). Tradition and change in urban schools: Curriculum, instruction, and assessment in action. In *Sociocultural studies and implications for science education* (pp. 155-173). Springer, Dordrecht.

- Rogers, R. D., & Monsell, S. (1995). Costs of a predictable switch between simple cognitive tasks. *Journal of experimental psychology: General, 124*(2), 207-231.

References

- Rousseau, D. M. (1990). New hire perceptions of their own and their employer's obligations: A study of psychological contracts. *Journal of Organizational Behavior, 11*(5), 389-400.

- Rust, R. T., & Huang, M. H. (2012). Optimizing service productivity. *Journal of Marketing, 76*(2), 47-66.

- Ryan, R. M., & Deci, E. L. (2000). Intrinsic and extrinsic motivations: Classic definitions and new directions. *Contemporary Educational Psychology, 25*(1), 54-67.

- Ryan, R. M., & Deci, E. L. (2000). Self-determination theory and the facilitation of intrinsic motivation, social development, and well-being. *American Psychologist, 55*(1), 68-78.

- Sackett, P. R. (2002). The structure of counterproductive work behaviors: Dimensionality and relationships with facets of job performance. *International Journal of Selection and Assessment, 10*(1-2), 5-11.

- Salancik, G. R., & Pfeffer, J. (1977). An examination of need-satisfaction models of job attitudes. *Administrative Science Quarterly, 22*(3), 427-456.

- Salas, E., Tannenbaum, S. I., Kraiger, K., & Smith-Jentsch, K. A. (2012). The science of training and development in organizations: What matters in practice. *Psychological Science in the Public Interest, 13*(2), 74-101.

- Salesforce (2019). *State of the Connected Customer*. Salesforce Research.

- Salovey, P., & Mayer, J. D. (1990). Emotional intelligence. *Imagination, Cognition, and Personality, 9*(3), 185-211.

- Sandikci, Ö., & Ger, G. (2007). Constructing and representing the Islamic consumer in Turkey. *Fashion Theory, 11*(2/3), 189-210.

- Schank, R. C., Berman, T. R., & Macpherson, K. A. (1999). Learning by doing. In *Instructional-design theories and models: A new paradigm of instructional theory* (Vol. 2, pp. 161-181). Lawrence Erlbaum Associates Publishers.

- Schein, E. H. (1978). *Career dynamics: Matching individual and organizational needs*. Addison-Wesley.

- Schein, E. H. (1985). *Organizational culture and leadership*. Jossey-Bass.

- Schein, E. H. (2010). *Organizational culture and leadership* (Vol. 2). John Wiley & Sons.

- Schmitt, B. (2003). *Customer experience management: A revolutionary approach to connecting with your customers*. John Wiley & Sons.

- Schön, D. A. (1983). *The reflective practitioner: How professionals think in action*. Basic books.

- Schön, D. A. (1983). *The reflective practitioner: How professionals think in action*. Basic books.

- Schön, D. A. (1987). Educating the reflective practitioner. Jossey-Bass.

References

- Schroeder, J. E. (2005). The artist and the brand. *European Journal of Marketing, 39*(11/12), 1291-1305.

- Schwartz, D. G., Farias, D. R., & Gerosa, M. A. (2017). A survey about methods and methodologies for evaluating groupware usability. *International Journal of Human–Computer Interaction, 33*(6), 465-484.

- Schwartz, J., & McCarthy, J. (2007). The shifting workforce: Scenarios for 2007. *Human Resource Planning, 30*(2), 5-12.

- Scott, J. C. (2001). *Domination and the arts of resistance: Hidden transcripts*. Yale University Press.

- Seibert, S. E., Kraimer, M. L., & Liden, R. C. (2001). A social capital theory of career success. *Academy of Management Journal, 44*(2), 219-237.

- Senge, P. M. (1990). *The fifth discipline: The art and practice of the learning organization*. Currency.

- Sherif, M. (1954). *Experimental study of positive and negative intergroup attitudes between experimentally produced groups: Robbers Cave study*. Norman, OK: University of Oklahoma, Institute of Group Relations.

- Shirky, C. (2008). *Here comes everybody: The power of organizing without organizations*. New York: Penguin Press.

- Sias, P. M. (2009). *Organizing relationships: Traditional and emerging perspectives on workplace relationships*. Sage Publications.

- Silverman, J., Kurtz, S., & Draper, J. (1996). *Skills for communicating with patients*. Radcliffe Publishing.

- Slepian, M. L., Ferber, S. N., Gold, J. M., & Rutchick, A. M. (2015). The cognitive consequences of formal clothing. *Social Psychological and Personality Science, 6*(6), 661-668.

- Smither, J. W. (Ed.). (1998). *Performance appraisal: State of the art in practice*. Jossey-Bass.

- Smither, J. W., London, M., & Reilly, R. R. (2005). Does performance improve following multisource feedback? A theoretical model, meta-analysis, and review of empirical findings. *Personnel Psychology, 58*(1), 33-66.

- Solomon, M. R., & Schopler, J. (1982). Self-consciousness and clothing. *Personality and Social Psychology Bulletin, 8*(3), 508-514.

- Sonnentag, S., Binnewies, C., & Mojza, E. J. (2010). Staying well and engaged when demands are high: The role of psychological detachment. *Journal of Applied Psychology, 95*(5), 965-976.

- Spector, P. E. (1994). Using self-report questionnaires in OB research: A comment on the use of a controversial method. *Journal of Organizational Behavior, 15*(5), 385-392.

- Stone, D. L. (2005). The boundaryless career: A new perspective for organizational inquiry. *Human Relations, 55*(1), 131-139.

- Stone, D. L., & Colella, A. (1996). A model of factors affecting the treatment of disabled individuals in organizations. *Academy of Management Review, 21*(2), 352-401.

References

- Stone, D., & Heen, S. (2014). *Thanks for the feedback: The science and art of receiving feedback well.* Penguin.

- Sullivan, S. E. (1999). The changing nature of careers: A review and research agenda. *Journal of Management, 25*(3), 457-484.

- Swanson, R. A., & Holton, E. F. (2009). *Foundations of human resource development.* Berrett-Koehler Publishers.

- Syed, J., & Kramar, R. (2010). What is the Australian model for managing cultural diversity? *Personnel Review, 39*(3), 373-391.

- Syed, J., & Özbilgin, M. (2009). A relational framework for international transfer of diversity management practices. *International Journal of Human Resource Management, 20*(12), 2435

- Tannenbaum, S. I., Beard, R. L., & Salas, E. (1992). Team building and its influence on team effectiveness: An examination of conceptual and empirical developments. *Issues, theory, and research in industrial/organizational psychology*, 82, 117-153.

- Taylor, F. W. (1911). *The principles of scientific management.* New York: Harper & Brothers.

- Taylor, W. C., Bitterman, M. I., & Brownson, R. C. (2012). Training needs and supports for evidence-based decision making among the public health workforce in the United States. *BMC Health Services Research, 12*(1), 1-9.

- Teece, D. J., Pisano, G., & Shuen, A. (1997). Dynamic capabilities and strategic management. *Strategic Management Journal, 18*(7), 509-533.

- Tharenou, P., Saks, A. M., & Moore, C. (2007). A review and critique of research on training and organizational-level outcomes. *Human Resource Management Review, 17*(3), 251-273.

- Thomas, D. A. (2001). The truth about mentoring minorities. Race matters. *Harvard Business Review, 79*(4), 98-112.

- Thomas, K. W., & Velthouse, B. A. (1990). Cognitive elements of empowerment: An "interpretive" model of intrinsic task motivation. *Academy of Management Review, 15*(4), 666-681.

- Tjosvold, D. (1985). Power and social context in superior-subordinate interaction. *Organizational Behavior and Human Decision Processes, 35*(3), 281-293.

- Tjosvold, D. (1991). The conflict-positive organization: It depends upon us. *Journal of Organizational Behavior, 12*(1), 19-28.

- Tjosvold, D. (2008). The conflict-positive organization: It depends upon us. *Journal of Organizational Behavior, 29*(1), 19-28.

- Tornow, W. W., & London, M. (1998). Maximizing the value of 360-degree feedback. Wiley.

- Trainor, K. J., Andzulis, J. M., Rapp, A., & Agnihotri, R. (2014). Social media technology usage and customer relationship performance: A capabilities-based examination of social CRM. *Journal of Business Research, 67*(6), 1201-1208.

- Tseëlon, E. (2001). *Masquerade and identities: Essays on gender, sexuality, and marginality*. Routledge.

References

- Tuckman, B. W. (1965). Developmental sequence in small groups. *Psychological Bulletin, 63*(6), 384.

- Tugade, M. M., & Fredrickson, B. L. (2004). Resilient individuals use positive emotions to bounce back from negative emotional experiences. *Journal of Personality and Social Psychology, 86*(2), 320-333.

- Turban, D. B., & Greening, D. W. (1997). Corporate social performance and organizational attractiveness to prospective employees. *Academy of Management Journal, 40*(3).

- Twenge, J. M. (2010). *A review of the empirical evidence on generational differences in work attitudes.* Journal of Business and Psychology, 25(2), 201-210.

- Uhl-Bien, M., & Arena, M. (2018). Complexity leadership: Enabling people and organizations for adaptability. *Organizational Dynamics, 47*(1), 8-20.

- Van Dijk, D., & Van Dick, R. (2009). Navigating organizational change: Change leaders, employee resistance and work-based identities. *Journal of Change Management, 9*(2), 143-163.

- Van Velsor, E., Taylor, S., & Leslie, J. B. (1993). An examination of the relationships among self-perception accuracy, self-awareness, gender, and leader effectiveness. *Human Resource Management, 32*(2-3), 249-264.

- Verhoef, P. C., Kannan, P. K., & Inman, J. J. (2015). From multi-channel retailing to omni-channel retailing: Introduction to the special issue on multi-channel retailing. *Journal of Retailing, 91*(2), 174-181.

- Verhoef, P. C., Neslin, S. A., & Vroomen, B. (2009). Multichannel customer management: Understanding the research-shopper phenomenon. *International Journal of Research in Marketing, 24*(2), 129-148.

- Wachtel, P. L. (1993). Therapeutic communication: Principles and effective practice. Guilford Press.

- Wageman, R. (1995). Interdependence and group effectiveness. *Administrative Science Quarterly, 40*(1), 145-180.

- Wajcman, J. (1998). Managing like a man: Women and men in corporate management. Penn State Press.

- Walther, J. B. (1996). Computer-mediated communication: Impersonal, interpersonal, and hyperpersonal interaction. *Communication Research, 23*(1), 3-43.

- Weber, M. (1922). *Economy and society*. University of California Press.

- Weger, H., Castle Bell, G., Minei, E. M., & Robinson, M. C. (2010). The relative effectiveness of active listening in initial interactions. *International Journal of Listening, 24*(1), 34-49.

- Wenger, E. (1998). *Communities of practice: Learning, meaning, and identity*. Cambridge University Press.

- Wenger, E. (2000). Communities of practice and social learning systems. *Organization, 7*(2), 225-246.

References

- Widmeyer, W. N., & Ducharme, K. (1997). Team building through team goal setting. _Journal of Applied Sport Psychology, 9_(1), 97-113.

- Wiederhold, B. K. (2020). Connecting through technology during the coronavirus disease 2019 pandemic: Avoiding "Zoom Fatigue." _Cyberpsychology, Behavior, and Social Networking, 23_(7), 437-438.

- Willis, J., & Todorov, A. (2006). First impressions: Making up your mind after a 100-ms exposure to a face. _Psychological Science, 17_(7), 592-598.

- Wolff, H. G., & Moser, K. (2009). Effects of networking on career success: A longitudinal study. _Journal of Applied Psychology, 94_(1), 196-206.

- World Health Organization. (2010). _Healthy workplaces: A model for action_. Geneva: WHO.

- Yukl, G. (2012). _Leadership in organizations_. Pearson.

- Zahn, G. L. (1991). Face-to-face communication in an office setting: The effects of position, proximity, and exposure. _Communication Research, 18_(6), 737-754.

- Zemke, R., Raines, C., & Filipczak, B. (2000). _Generations at work: Managing the clash of Veterans, Boomers, Xers, and Nexters in your workplace_. AMACOM.

- Zhang, B., Daugherty, T., & Enberg, C. (2019). How do your customers really feel? Leveraging chatbots and virtual assistants to capture real-time emotions. _Business Horizons, 62_(1), 83-93.

- Zimmerman, B. J. (2002). Becoming a self-regulated learner: An overview. *Theory into Practice, 41*(2), 64-70.

- Zimmerman, B. J. (2008). Investigating self-regulation and motivation: Historical background, methodological developments, and future prospects. *American Educational Research Journal, 45*(1), 166-183.

- Zuboff, S. (2019). *The age of surveillance capitalism: The fight for a human future at the new frontier of power.* PublicAffairs.